Literacy

LOOK-FORS

An Observation Protocol to Guide K–6 Classroom Walkthroughs

Elaine K. McEwan-Adkins

Solution Tree | Press

a division of

Solution Tree

555 North Morton Street
Bloomington, IN 47404

800.733.6786 (toll free) / 812.336.7700
FAX: 812.336.7790

email: info@solution-tree.com
solution-tree.com

Visit **go.solution-tree.com/literacy** to download the reproducibles in this book.

Printed in the United States of America
15   14   13   12   11   1   2   3   4   5

FSC
Mixed Sources
Product group from well-managed forests and other controlled sources
Cert no. SW-COC-002283
www.fsc.org
© 1996 Forest Stewardship Council

Library of Congress Cataloging-in-Publication Data

McEwan-Adkins, Elaine K., 1941-
  Literacy look-fors : an observation protocol to guide K-6 classroom walkthroughs / Elaine K. McEwan-Adkins.
       p. cm.
  Includes bibliographical references and index.
  ISBN 978-1-935542-18-6 (perfect bound) -- ISBN 978-1-935542-19-3 (library edition) 1. Language arts (Elementary) I. Title.
  LB1576.M195 2011
  372.6--dc22
                                        2011015764

Solution Tree
Jeffrey C. Jones, CEO & President

Solution Tree Press
President: Douglas M. Rife
Publisher: Robert D. Clouse
Vice President of Production: Gretchen Knapp
Managing Production Editor: Caroline Wise
Proofreader: Rachel Rosolina
Text Designer: Amy Shock
Cover Designer: Jenn Taylor

To Salli Mahaffy, whose questions about what to look for during classroom walkthroughs inspired this book.

Acknowledgments

Solution Tree Press would like to thank the following reviewers:

Kathleen Douglas
District Instructional Coach
Fort Wayne Community Schools
Fort Wayne, Indiana

Sherrilyn Duquette
Assistant Principal
Conway Middle School
Conway, South Carolina

Laurie Elish-Piper
Presidential Teaching Professor,
Department of Literacy Education
Northern Illinois University
DeKalb, Illinois

Christine Hoffman
Principal
Inverness Elementary School
Birmingham, Alabama

Jane Moore
Assistant Principal
Jerry Junkins Elementary
Dallas, Texas

Maryann Mraz
Associate Professor, Department of
Reading and Elementary Education
University of North Carolina at
Charlotte
Charlotte, North Carolina

Visit **go.solution-tree.com/literacy** to download the reproducibles in this book.

Table of Contents

Chapter 1

Chapter 2

Understand the Classroom Walkthroughs 47

Chapter 3

Assess Your Instructional Leadership Capacity 59

Chapter 4
Orient Your Faculty to the Look-Fors and Walkthroughs

Chapter 5
Collect and Analyze Look-For Frequency Data

About the Author

Elaine K. McEwan-Adkins, EdD, is a partner and educational consultant with the McEwan-Adkins Group, offering professional development in literacy and school leadership. A former teacher, librarian, principal, and assistant superintendent for instruction in several suburban Chicago school districts, Dr. McEwan-Adkins was honored by the Illinois Principals Association as an outstanding instructional leader, by the Illinois State Board of Education with an Award of Excellence in the Those Who Excel Program, and by the National Association of Elementary School Principals as the 1991 National Distinguished Principal from Illinois.

Dr. McEwan-Adkins is the author of more than thirty-five books for parents and educators. Her most recent titles include *40 Reading Intervention Strategies for K–6 Students: Research-Based Support for RTI, Teach Them All to Read,* and *Ten Traits of Highly Effective Schools.*

She received an undergraduate degree in education from Wheaton College and a master's degree in library science and a doctorate in educational administration from Northern Illinois University.

To book Elaine McEwan-Adkins for professional development, contact pd@solution-tree.com.

Preface

Literacy is the foundation of learning and achievement at every educational level and in every stage of life thereafter. As students move through elementary school, ideally they are acquiring solid literacy skills that enable them to read increasingly more challenging texts and write in more advanced and sophisticated ways. In order to realize this goal for *all* students, their administrators, literacy leaders, and instructional coaches need the knowledge and skills to simultaneously assess and build instructional capacity—the collective abilities of a school staff to teach all students to read and write to specified standards of achievement, irrespective of their demographics or categorical labels.

My Goal in Writing This Book

My goal in writing this book is to make a positive impact on literacy levels in elementary schools. I have been working on that goal for more than twenty-five years—first as a principal raising literacy attainment in a low-achieving school, then as an assistant superintendent for instruction, and finally as an author and consultant in the United States and Canada. You may wonder what keeps me motivated.

The answer is simple: I have grandchildren and great-grandchildren who have yet to enter kindergarten, and I want the schools in which they enroll to provide them with the opportunities *they* need in order to learn to read and write at the highest possible levels. I believe all students (irrespective of their demographics or any labels that might have been affixed to them as early as preschool or kindergarten) deserve the opportunity to learn in the context of a balanced literacy program taught by highly effective teachers at every grade level. Unfortunately, there are too many schools where educators point to inalterable demographic variables as the cause of low literacy levels, other schools where key components of a balanced literacy program are missing, and still others where a critical mass of unsupported and untrained teachers contribute to depressed instructional capacity. My goal is to provide the motivation, encouragement, knowledge, and skills that all elementary school educators need to build not only the instructional capacities of their schools, but also the academic and leadership capacities.

What This Book Is

Literacy Look-Fors: An Observation Protocol to Guide K–6 Classroom Walkthroughs is a practical, research-based resource that addresses two of the biggest challenges facing elementary school literacy leaders today:

1. How can I acquire the knowledge I need to become an effective literacy leader?

2. How can I become more purposeful and focused in conducting classroom walkthroughs?

The literacy look-fors observation protocol is a formative whole-school instructional capacity assessment containing sixty research-based indicators. It is designed to guide your classroom walkthroughs during the literacy block. It will also enable you to assess the extent to which professional development and literacy coaching initiatives in your school and district are making an impact on instruction, and will suggest what types of embedded professional development programs may be needed for individuals, grade levels, or the entire faculty.

What This Book Is Not

There is a risk in giving any group of educators a list—especially one with sixty items. In the hands of those looking for easy answers, any defined set of indicators can quickly become a classroom inspection form or a teacher evaluation instrument. The literacy look-fors observation protocol is not meant to serve either of these purposes. It is designed to help you, an administrator, coach, or literacy leader, focus your classroom walkthroughs, assess the instructional capacity of your school, and then inform the development of embedded professional growth, particularly the kinds of activities that take place in collaborative grade-level literacy teams. The data you collect during your walkthroughs can guide your selection of professional resources, dictate the types of whole-school professional growth activities you plan, and inform the budget you build to foster professional growth in your staff, but in reality, the sixty look-fors are only an appetizer for what I hope will be a gourmet adventure of literacy learning for you and your staff. I am not so naïve as to think that the look-fors have everything you and your teachers need. What they can provide is a place to begin if you want to build a balanced literacy program in your school.

The Audience for This Book

The primary audience for this book consists of individual elementary school principals and assistant principals, literacy coaches, and literacy leaders. The following individuals may also benefit from the book's schoolwide approach to building instructional capacity:

❏ School leadership teams could use the book to undertake an assessment of the instructional capacity of their schools. When examined along with formative and summative school achievement data, look-for frequency data will point to areas schoolwide in which instructional and curricular improvements are needed and will target where professional development is needed.

❏ Teams of specialized teachers such as Title I teachers, interventionists, diagnosticians, literacy coaches, psychologists, or speech pathologists could use this book as a way to notch up their collective instructional capacity and improve their services to teachers.

❏ Individual specialized teachers such as those listed in the previous bullet could use this book as a basis for tailoring presentations and professional growth experiences for the teachers with whom they work.

❏ Some schools are dealing with high teacher turnover, large numbers of novice or alternatively certified teachers, or a critical mass of teachers with low confidence and knowledge levels. Administrators and literacy coaches in these schools could use this book to assess instructional capacity and design an in-house professional growth experience that is targeted to one of these high-needs groups.

❏ In schools in which administrators, literacy coaches, and teacher teams are already using classroom walkthroughs to focus instructional and curricular discussions between and among staff, the literacy look-fors will bring a more specialized perspective to their observations and professional growth experiences.

Embedded Professional Growth Opportunities

As you begin to use the literacy look-fors observation protocol to guide your classroom walkthroughs, you will become more attuned to the needs of your staff for embedded professional growth opportunities that are directly connected to the learning needs of your students. You may then wish to investigate my companion book for teachers, *Collaborative Teacher Literacy Teams:*

Connecting Professional Growth and Student Achievement (McEwan-Adkins, in press). It contains twenty professional growth units, each with a built-in Leader's Guide. The units are based on the literacy look-fors and connect teachers' professional growth to academic goals in the classroom.

Just ahead, the introduction contains important background knowledge and information about the literacy look-fors observation protocol and how to use it in your school. In your eagerness to get started, you may be tempted to fast-forward to chapter 1, but take the time needed to become familiar with the unique vocabulary and organizational structure of the observation protocol. The success of your implementation depends on a solid understanding of the literacy look-fors.

Introduction

Ultimately, improving [the literacy attainment of] schools depends on working harder, increasing efficiency, and building capacity for more powerful instruction.

—Hatch (2009, p. 32)

Literacy Look-Fors: An Observation Protocol to Guide K–6 Classroom Walkthroughs is about increasing your school's capacity for delivering more powerful literacy instruction. Delivering balanced literacy instruction encompasses selecting what to teach (such as phonemic awareness, word identification skills, or comprehension strategies), how to teach it (with direct teacher-managed instruction or indirect student-managed learning), and in what setting to teach it (whole group, small group, individually, or cooperatively), to create what Michael Pressley calls "instruction that is more than the sum of its parts" (Pressley, 1998, p. 1). Balanced literacy instruction enables all students to attain literacy standards that are at grade level or higher. Some students will need ongoing scaffolding from their classroom teachers during small-group interventions to keep up with grade-level instruction. Students with reading disabilities will need more intensive instruction in specialized curricula to become literate. Still other students will need enrichment that includes reading more difficult text, writing about it in more sophisticated ways, "teaching" their classmates about what they have learned, and becoming self-directed readers and writers.

When my now-adult daughter enrolled in kindergarten, her teacher determined very early that she and four of her classmates already knew how to read. The teacher formed a small group and targeted instruction to those students' needs during the remainder of the school year. When my son enrolled two years later with the same teacher, she determined that *he* needed phonics instruction as a staple of his balanced literacy diet. My children have identical IQs and both ultimately earned PhDs, but that information would have been irrelevant to their highly effective kindergarten teacher, even if she could have foretold the future. Her goal was to keep every student on track to become a fluent reader by the end of second grade, and to accomplish that goal she "bal-anced" the needs of individual students, the literacy content, and her instruc-tional approaches.

The Roadblocks to Teaching All Students to Read and Write

Joe Torgesen (2006) identified the biggest roadblock to on-grade-level lit-eracy attainment for all students: "We will never teach all of our students to read if we do not teach our students who have the greatest difficulties to read. Another way to say this is: Getting to 100 percent requires going through the bottom 20 percent" (p. 1). There are few educators who would argue about the desirability of teaching all students to read and write. However, there are far too many who have simply written off the bottom 20 percent of students in their schools. These educators believe that they are already working as hard as they can and simply cannot do any more than they already have.

During the past twenty-five years, reformers including state departments of education, boards of education, central office administrators, school prin-cipals, a wide variety of private organizations and institutions, and even the federal government have tried multiple approaches to tackling the "can'ts and the won'ts" of literacy instruction, with varying degrees of success. The initiatives have included all-school reform models, improved research-based reading programs, instructional leadership training for principals, profes-sional development for teachers, literacy leaders to coach teachers, profes-sional learning communities to build collective knowledge and accountability, performance-based bonuses to motivate educators to try harder, and failing grades on accountability report cards for schools that don't make sufficient progress. We undeniably know more today about what constitutes balanced literacy instruction than we ever have. However, my conclusions regarding one of the root causes of low literacy levels today, especially for some groups of students, are not unlike those I drew during my first week as a novice prin-cipal. Although I had no prior experience working in low-achieving schools, I knew with certainty that the students and parents were not to blame for this depressing state of affairs.

The biggest problem was ineffective instruction in nearly half of the school's classrooms. This sad truth was compounded by the total absence of any content standards or program alignment and a casual approach to allocat-ing and using time. Even the Herculean efforts of a few outstanding teachers seemed to vanish in a morass of marginal instruction. Extreme teacher isola-tion and low trust levels further exacerbated low achievement levels—reading achievement overall in grades 2–6 hovered at the 20th percentile on the standardized test that was given yearly. It was no mystery why the instructional and academic capacities of this school had nearly run dry—lack of instructional leadership.

As we collaboratively increased the school's instructional and leadership capacities by sharing the load and assuming collective responsibilities for all of our students, our academic capacity rose to the 70th and 80th percentiles in reading. Our English learners and high-poverty students not only learned to read, but they were also motivated to read at school, at home, and during summer vacations. It took eight years, and our learning curve was steep. In spite of how hard we worked, we did not have the knowledge and skills to meet the needs of our bottom 20 to 30 percent of students.

Although educators today face similar demographics to those in my student body, there is one big difference: today, there *are* research-based solutions. However, the biggest challenge still facing elementary school educators is how to build sufficient instructional capacity to teach all students to read and write to a grade-level standard.

Key Concepts

This book introduces numerous concepts that may be unfamiliar to you and some terms defined in ways that may be different from their common usage in discussions of literacy. Figure I.1 provides definitions for these key concepts as they are used in this book.

Figure I.1: Definitions of Key Concepts

Term	Definition
Balanced Literacy	The implementation of targeted programs and instruction that results in on-grade-level or higher levels of literacy achievement for all students, irrespective of their demographics or categorical labels
Instructional Capacity	The collective abilities of the teachers in a given school to teach and get results for all students
Instructional Leadership Capacity	The collective abilities of the administrators and teacher leaders to build and maintain a professional learning community and solve problems of teaching and learning to move toward the goal of success for all students
Academic Capacity	The collective abilities of all students to learn—and demonstrate their learning—in relevant and rigorous work products (daily assignments, writing projects, problem-solving tasks, and group projects) as well as in the results of formative and summative assessments

continued →

Term	Definition
Literacy Look-Fors Observation Protocol	A set of research-based exemplars of effective literacy instruction
Literacy Look-For	A research-based characteristic, action, or attitude of a teacher or student; a condition or climate in the classroom; or an artifact created by a teacher or student during literacy instruction that is critical to that instruction
"Little Look-Fors"	A group of more specific or detailed look-fors that would fall into a category headed by the one of the literacy look-fors
Indicator or Exemplar	Used interchangeably to refer to the literacy look-fors that are a part of the observation protocol
Nonexemplar	The ineffective implementation of a look-for or the opposite of an indicator or exemplar
Protocol	A set of recommended practices that are known to achieve certain types of results; in education, a set of research-based behaviors that, when employed by teachers, results in literacy learning that is significantly higher than when these behaviors are absent (a protocol can be considered a type of rubric or continuum of quality or completeness against which educators can assess the instructional capacity of their school for effective literacy instruction)
Principal Classroom Walkthrough	A two- to three-minute classroom scan by the principal to collect frequency data on one or more literacy look-fors from the literacy look-fors observation protocol
Teacher Team Classroom Walkthrough	A two- to three-minute classroom scan by a grade-level team to look for indicators or exemplars that have been the focus of embedded professional development in collaborative team meetings
Debriefing	A thirty-minute meeting in which the principal, coach, or team leader and a grade-level team debrief about what they have observed during their classroom walkthroughs
Learning Stems	A set of prompts for teachers to initially use in their thirty-minute debriefing meeting after classroom walkthroughs
Checksheet	The data collection form principals use to collect frequency data
Frequency Data	The number of times that a certain literacy look-for is observed in classrooms during a one-month period; for example, if scaffolding is observed in fifteen classrooms during three out of the four walkthroughs, the frequency of scaffolding would be 45 out of 60 (note that a look-for can be counted only once per scan in a classroom)
Collaborative Teacher Team	A teacher work group (often called a professional learning community) having the characteristics of trust, self-reflection, support, communication, shared mission, and conflict resolution skills; the shared purpose and collaborative activity build collective responsibility among grade-level team members

Term	Definition
Professional Growth Unit	A set of learning activities designed to provide embedded professional development about a specific literacy topic
Collaborative Planning Time	The time dedicated to collaborative work around shared goals focused on teaching and learning in a grade-level team
Embedded Professional Development	Professional development that is directly related to the specific needs and goals of a grade-level team or a whole school faculty and is carried on or acted upon in a collaborative team meeting; in the early context of this book, *embedded professional development* refers to each grade-level team working collaboratively to unpack one literacy look-for
Experimental and Quasi-Experimental Research	Research in which there is a treatment group (of students, schools, teachers, or other units) that participates in an intervention and is then compared to a control group that does not receive the intervention; in experimental research, the students, schools, teachers, or other units are randomly assigned to either the treatment group or the control group; in quasi-experimental research, there is no random assignment, and researchers must control for the various possibilities that it was not the treatment that made the difference, but some other preexisting variable
Correlational Research	Nonexperimental research in which it is nearly impossible to determine whether a particular variable "caused" changes in another variable; correlational research does not have randomized assignment of teachers, students, or schools to treatment and control groups and therefore must be carefully examined to see whether researchers have employed statistical controls to compensate and must include a thorough discussion of how and why the results might be biased
Cognitive Strategies	Mental processes or physical acts that readers employ during reading and writing to aid in the understanding and retention of text; this term is used interchangeably with the term *comprehension strategies* for the purpose of helping the reader understand (generally, *comprehension strategies* can refer to just about anything a teacher teaches during literacy instruction, whereas the seven cognitive strategies of high skilled readers—activating, inferring, monitoring-clarifying, questioning, searching-selecting, summarizing, and visualizing-organizing—are research-based and must be directly instructed [McEwan, 2006])

*Visit **go.solution-tree.com/literacy** to download and print this figure.*

Understanding the look-fors and how they act and interact to produce literacy achievement at various grade levels is important, but merely knowing a lot about literacy instruction will not grant you and your teachers the power to achieve the literacy goals that are the centerpiece of your school improvement plan. It is the consistent, coherent, and coordinated *implementation* of those literacy look-fors in every classroom that holds the power to bring all students to grade level or well above when it comes to literacy attainment. As the instructional leader, the only way you can really determine if your literacy implementation is on target is by taking daily classroom walkthroughs to collect formative frequency data to assess your school's instructional capacity.

The Steps to Implementing the Look-fors and Walkthroughs

The seven chapters in this book will walk you through the implementation process step by step. Figure I.2 graphically displays the school-changing journey you and your staff will take together as you collaboratively discover how to notch up literacy instruction in your school.

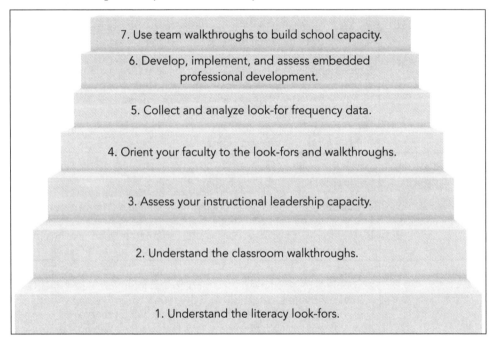

7. Use team walkthroughs to build school capacity.

6. Develop, implement, and assess embedded professional development.

5. Collect and analyze look-for frequency data.

4. Orient your faculty to the look-fors and walkthroughs.

3. Assess your instructional leadership capacity.

2. Understand the classroom walkthroughs.

1. Understand the literacy look-fors.

Figure I.2: Seven Steps to Effective Implementation

Visit go.solution-tree.com/literacy to download and print this figure.

Chapter 1: Understand the Literacy Look-Fors

Your first step is to personally understand the five categories of literacy look-fors. Once you have a clear picture of these categories, you can begin to focus on the discrete look-fors that make up each category. To assist you in your understanding, you will find three figures for each category of look-fors: (1) a literacy look-fors observation protocol; (2) a set of citations showing how various look-fors impact student learning; and (3) a set of exemplars and nonexemplars. As you consider the sixty look-fors, keep in mind that each one describes an exemplar, a model, or an ideal on which teachers can model their instruction. You will also find a nonexemplar for each look-for—the polar opposite of the ideal. They are there to help you become more discriminating about the presence of the look-fors as you conduct your classroom walkthroughs.

Chapter 2: Understand the Classroom Walkthroughs

The second step to a successful implementation of the look-fors and walkthroughs is to become familiar with the walkthroughs model featured in this book and determine how it differs from other walkthrough models. You will also find answers to the questions most often asked by principals before, during, and after their implementation.

Chapter 3: Assess Your Instructional Leadership Capacity

This chapter will help you assess your instructional leadership capacity using two different instruments. It also presents some roadblocks you may encounter during the implementation process.

Chapter 4: Orient Your Faculty to the Look-Fors and Walkthroughs

This chapter provides a three-part orientation program. However, since you know your teachers, the culture of your school, your teacher contract, and any past history that may impact the implementation of the look-fors and walkthroughs, you may wish to customize an orientation to better meet the needs of your staff. During one of your orientation meetings, you will lead your staff through a process to select the literacy look-fors you will use in your first set of walkthroughs in chapter 5.

Chapter 5: Collect and Analyze Look-For Frequency Data

Once your faculty has been oriented to the look-fors and walkthroughs, you will begin a one-month collection of baseline data using the small set of look-fors you selected with your faculty in chapter 4. Collecting look-for data is a surprisingly easy process that will take between fifteen to thirty minutes per day depending on the number of classrooms in your school. You will need only one or two pieces of paper, a clipboard, and some colored markers. Continually remind yourself and reassure your teachers that classroom walkthroughs are designed to collect frequency data, not evaluate teachers. This chapter will provide directions for collating, aggregating, and analyzing the data from your first month. You will then present these aggregated data to the faculty and move forward to discuss what the data mean and how to design embedded professional development to meet a need revealed by the data.

Chapter 6: Develop, Implement, and Assess Embedded Professional Development

At this point, you are ready to consider the kind of professional growth opportunities your staff may need, based on your analysis of the data in chapter 5. There are six phases to the step in this chapter:

1. Share the results of frequency data collection with your literacy team, and select the look-for to be the focus of embedded (PD) professional development.

2. Share the results of frequency data collection with teachers, and identify the look-for selected by the literacy team.

3. Model the look-for unpacking process for faculty, and describe the summarizing activity to be presented to the staff at the close of the embedded PD experience.

4. Hold a meeting at which each team presents its summarizer.

5. Facilitate the development of student achievement goals at each grade level.

6. Engage in a follow-up month of frequency data collection to evaluate the implementation.

Chapter 7: Use Team Walkthroughs to Build School Capacity

As you become more skilled in using the cycle of assessing your school's instructional capacity and developing targeted and embedded professional growth opportunities, encourage your faculty to take on additional responsibilities for conducting literacy walkthroughs, presenting and modeling teaching for colleagues, and designing embedded professional growth units that meet teachers' assessed needs.

Figure I.3 presents a recommended timeline for implementing the seven steps. It is your decision regarding when to begin and how quickly to move, based on the demands already placed on you and your staff. The suggested timeline allows adequate time for a faithful implementation of look-fors and walkthroughs in your school. When one is introduced to a new concept or model for improving student achievement, there is always the temptation to want to get it up and running as quickly as possible. Some will think in terms of taking a Friday to orient the faculty to the whole process so they can begin implementing on Monday. I have been there and done that. Shortcutting orientation meetings and not giving teachers adequate time to think and learn together greatly reduces the likelihood of a successful implementation.

Figure I.3: Suggested Implementation Timeline

Implementation Steps	Suggested Time for Implementation	Specifics of Required Meetings
Steps 1–3: Understand the look-fors and walkthroughs, and assess your personal instructional leadership capacity.	This should take one to two months.	You could choose to have small meetings with a leadership group to study the look-fors and walkthroughs. If you choose to study with your peers, you will be asked to select a literacy leadership group to assist in Step 6.
Step 4: Orient the faculty.	Three meetings should be held over a one-month period of time.	These meetings could be held during a regularly scheduled faculty meeting or during an early release day dedicated to professional development.
Step 5: Collect and analyze look-fors frequency data.	One month should include four visits in each classroom during the literacy block to collect frequency data.	There will be no meetings as you collect and analyze the data. You could choose to meet with a small building leadership team to assist you in analyzing the look-for data.
Step 6a: Share the results of frequency data collection with your literacy team, and select the literacy look-for that will be the focus of embedded PD.	As soon as possible after you have collected, aggregated, and analyzed the data, hold this meeting. You will want to maintain momentum at this point.	Step 6a consists of one meeting. Do not move on to Step 6b until you have this first meeting.
Step 6b: Share the results of frequency data collection with teachers, and identify the look-for selected by the literacy team.	If this discussion is a particularly long one or you sense some resistance from faculty members, take time to get around those roadblocks before moving to Step 6c.	If this meeting goes quickly, you may wish to move immediately to Step 6c.

continued →

Implementation Steps	Suggested Time for Implementation	Specifics of Required Meetings
Step 6c: Model the look-for unpacking process for faculty, and describe the summarizing activity to take place after implementation.	The timelines for this step depend on how often and for what period of time teachers have to work through their embedded PD project. At a minimum, they should have three meetings that are between forty-five and sixty minutes long. I don't recommend you expect staff to hold these meetings on their own time unless your staff has come to you volunteering to this.	Take time to drop in on all of the grade-level teams while they are engaged in their unpacking project, remind them of the required summarizing project, and encourage and affirm the work they are doing.
Step 6d: Hold a meeting to hear the summarizing presentations from each team.	If you have one team that is stuck, talk it over with them to determine what the problem may be, and let them know that if they are not prepared by the time of the announced meeting date, the rest of the teams will present and they will be on the next faculty meeting agenda in a solo performance.	
Step 6e: Facilitate the development of student achievement goals at each grade level, and set a date (twenty student attendance days from the beginning date) to report on the goal achievement.	This will likely take a full calendar month or longer if there are one- or two-day holidays that interrupt the school calendar. Make sure that whatever "treatment" a team is providing, their students have a full twenty days to take advantage of it.	Drop in on team meetings during this period to find out how they are progressing. Let them know that you are monitoring and that you are available if they need help or resources.
Step 6f: Engage in a follow-up frequency data collection to determine the effectiveness of the embedded PD and the student achievement goals.	This process will take a full calendar month or longer depending on the school calendar.	Remember to once again emphasize to teachers that you are collecting frequency data to evaluate the collective instructional capacity of the school.

Implementation Steps	Suggested Time for Implementation	Specifics of Required Meetings
Step 7: Conduct team walkthroughs.	This will take between one and two months.	There will be one meeting to review the team walkthroughs process with faculty. Although they received the guidelines and learning stems at their orientation meeting, they will need a thorough review and a time for questions to be answered.
The total elapsed time from beginning of implementation to the conclusion of the initial team walkthroughs should be nine to ten months overall.		

The Next Step

In chapter 1, you will gain an understanding of the literacy look-fors and how they look in the classrooms of highly effective teachers so you can find them in your school classrooms.

Chapter 1

Understand the Literacy Look-Fors

[The educator must] be a scholar, an intellectual, and a knowledge worker oriented toward the interpretation, communication, and construction of such knowledge in the interests of student learning.

—Shulman (1999, p. xiii)

1. **Understand the literacy look-fors.**
2. Understand the classroom walkthroughs.
3. Assess your instructional leadership capacity.
4. Orient your faculty to the look-fors and walkthroughs.
5. Collect and analyze look-for frequency data.
6. Develop, implement, and assess embedded professional development.
7. Use team walkthroughs to build school capacity.

The first step to a successful implementation of the look-fors and walkthroughs is to gain a solid understanding of the literacy look-fors. This chapter assumes that you are in a leadership capacity in an elementary school and that you are eager to become more knowledgeable about literacy instruction. Those who intend to use the literacy look-fors observation protocol to build capacity in their schools, such as administrators, literacy coaches, and instructional supervisors, will want to master the definitions and critical attributes of the look-fors so they can immediately recognize them during classroom walkthroughs. The ease with which you acquire the knowledge in this chapter will depend on your background knowledge, the time you have available to study and learn, and the degree to which you are able to process this information with administrative colleagues and learn from highly effective staff members. If you have no prior experience with elementary literacy instruction, little available time, and few knowledgeable colleagues, the process will take longer. However, nothing is impossible if you are motivated. Your first task is to acquire an understanding of the literacy look-fors.

A helpful way to understand and ultimately remember the sixty look-fors without the printed list is by thinking of them in their five categories (shown in figure 1.1). These categories are unique to my work and are based on qualitative and quantitative literacy and instructional effectiveness research with special emphasis on look-fors that are shown by research to positively impact student achievement.

Figure 1.1: The Five Categories of Literacy Look-Fors

Category	Description
Instructional Moves	Instructional moves are the positive and purpose-driven actions, attitudes, and words that highly effective teachers use to communicate with students during literacy instruction.
Teacher-Managed Instructional Activities	Teacher-managed instructional activities are lessons in which teachers provide targeted, direct, explicit, systematic, supportive instruction to students in any of the eight curricular components of a balanced literacy program.
Teacher With-It-Ness Components	Teacher with-it-ness is the state of being on top of, tuned in to, aware of, and in complete control of the various organizational and management facets of classroom life. With-it-ness also includes the ability to preview, project, and predict the challenges and contingencies of an upcoming school year and the expertise to proactively design and teach a set of expectations (routines, rubrics, and rules) during the first three weeks of school.
Student-Managed Learning Activities	Student-managed learning activities are those for which students have acquired the necessary skills and strategies to independently manage and complete a wide range of literacy tasks to include reading, writing, presenting, consulting, and teaching.
Classroom Artifacts	Classroom artifacts are: (1) physical objects in the classroom (posters, signs, agendas, assignment notebooks, vocabulary and reading logs, and rubrics), (2) teacher-developed written documents that enable teachers to use their walls and boards as "teaching assistants" and motivators, and (3) student-produced written documents such as work displayed in the classroom, homework assignments, and work produced during teacher-managed instruction or student-managed learning activities that give evidence of rigor and relevance.

*Visit **go.solution-tree.com/literacy** to download and print this figure.*

Just ahead you will find an explanatory section for each of the categories in figure 1.1. Each section contains an observation protocol with brief definitions of the category's look-fors, an explanation of the category's "big idea," a set of research citations, and a chart describing nonexemplars that contrast with the look-fors in the category. For a complete set of the literacy look-fors observation protocol containing the sixty look-fors and their definitions, see figure 1.1.1 at **go.solution-tree.com/literacy**. For a complete set of the exemplars and nonexemplars for the sixty look-fors see figure 1.1.2 at **go.solution-tree.com/literacy**.

Literacy Look-Fors: Instructional Moves

Instructional moves are positive and purpose-driven actions, attitudes, and words that highly effective teachers use to communicate with students during literacy instruction. Although instructional moves can be employed at any grade level and for teaching any content area, we will examine them solely in the context of elementary school literacy instruction. I developed this list of moves based on the findings of multiple qualitative classroom observation studies of literacy instruction (Bogner, Raphael, & Pressley, 2002; Foorman, Francis, Fletcher, Schatschneider, & Mehta, 1998; Kern & Clemens, 2007; McCutchen et al., 2002; Pressley, El-Dinary, Gaskins, et al., 1992; Pressley, Wharton-McDonald, Allington, et al., 2001; Pressley, Wharton-McDonald, Raphael, et al., 2001; Stichter, Stormont, & Lewis, 2009; Taylor, Pearson, Clark, & Walpole, 2000; Wharton-McDonald, Pressley, & Hampston, 1998). Figure 1.2 contains the literacy look-fors observation protocol for instructional moves.

Figure 1.2: Look-Fors Observation Protocol—Instructional Moves

Activating-Connecting	The teacher generates interest in learning, activates prior knowledge, and connects instruction to the real world or to the solution of real problems.
Affirming-Appreciating	The teacher appreciates, encourages, praises, or rewards students' actions, attitudes, thinking processes, verbal statements, and work products. The praise is specific and focuses on excellent work products as well as improvements in students' thinking and efforts.
Annotating	The teacher adds additional information while reading text together with students or during a group discussion—information that students do not have, but need in order to make sense of the discussion or text. The teacher builds background and vocabulary knowledge as often as possible using relevant examples from students' experiences.
Assessing	The teacher determines both formally (through testing) and informally (through questioning) what students have learned and where instruction needs to be differentiated for all students to achieve mastery.

continued →

Attributing	The teacher communicates to students that their accomplishments are the result of effort, wise decision making, attending to the task, and exercising good judgment and perseverance, rather than intelligence or ability.
Coaching-Facilitating	The teacher thinks along with students and helps them develop their own ideas, rather than directing their thinking and telling them what to do.
Constructing	The teacher and students work collaboratively to construct multiple meanings from conversations, discussions, and the reading of text.
Differentiating	The teacher calibrates the difficulty of learning tasks so as to create the best match with students' assessed skills and knowledge.
Directly Instructing	The teacher uses a direct, explicit, systematic, and supportive approach to teaching.
Explaining	The teacher tells students what will happen in a lesson, what the goal is, why it's important, how it will help students, and what the roles of the teacher and students will be during the lesson.
Giving Directions	The teacher gives clear and concise verbal instructions (supported by written directions, picture cues, or modeling as needed) that help students see how they are going to get from where they are at the beginning of a lesson, task, or unit to the completion of the task or outcome.
Grouping	The teacher uses benchmark assessment results to group and re-group students according to their specific academic needs for scaffolded instruction, enrichment, or specialized interventions.
Guiding Practice	The teacher leads students through a supervised rehearsal of a skill, process, or routine to ensure understanding, accuracy, and automaticity.
Modeling	The teacher thinks aloud regarding the cognitive processing of text and physically represents that thinking by constructing graphic organizers or writing in response to reading while students observe.
Motivating	The teacher encourages, inspires, and stimulates students to achieve both personal and group goals by scaffolding instruction, affirming academic efforts, and providing extrinsic rewards as needed to jump-start struggling students.
Nurturing-Mentoring	The teacher communicates positive expectations, exhibits a caring attitude, and takes a personal interest in the success of students.
Questioning	The teacher uses a variety of questioning techniques and types of questions to stimulate students' thinking, while also teaching students how to ask and answer their own questions.
Recapping	The teacher summarizes what has been concluded, learned, or constructed during a given lesson or discussion and tells students why this new learning is important and where they can apply it in the future.

Redirecting	The teacher monitors the level of student attention and engagement and uses a variety of techniques, prompts, and signals to regain or redirect students' attention to the learning task.
Reminding	The teacher causes students to remember or think more deeply about an idea or concept that has been previously taught or restates something that has been previously taught in a novel way to ensure their remembering.
Reteaching	The teacher teaches recursively by repeatedly coming back to important skills, concepts, outcomes, or standards, giving students multiple opportunities to achieve mastery.
Scaffolding	The teacher provides instructional support at students' independent learning levels enabling them to solve problems, carry out tasks, master content and skills, utilize appropriate cognitive strategies, and generally achieve goals that would otherwise be impossible.

*Visit **go.solution-tree.com/literacy** to download and print this figure.*

The Big Idea of Instructional Moves

The big idea of this category is *instructional moves are purpose-driven*. Each move, when executed in a research-based way, accomplishes a specific goal. Consider, for example, the first instructional move, assessing. Assessing *prior to instruction* enables teachers to gauge where their students are on the continuum to mastery and provides information teachers need to target lessons to the precise needs of their students. Assessing *during* instruction enables teachers to make mid-lesson corrections, while assessing *after a lesson has been taught* enables teachers to both determine the effectiveness of their instruction and also provide feedback to students on their performance and progress.

Assessing for *grading*, on the other hand, is far less positive and purpose-driven, often signifying to students that teachers are finished teaching a skill or unit and are moving on, regardless of how many students they may be leaving behind. Even less positive and purpose-driven is the unfortunate practice of simply assessing for *record keeping*, collecting student assessment data that gather dust on your desk or take up memory on your hard drive.

Almost any of the instructional move look-fors listed in figure 1.2 can be executed in unplanned and purposeless ways that result in wasted allocated time. During my early classroom walkthroughs as a new elementary school principal, I discovered a wide range of teacher effectiveness. Teacher A was an exemplar of every instructional move in the look-fors. She had a rationale for every statement she made, a reason for every example she selected, and an underlying principle for every word of affirmation she gave to individual students. Even her decisions about where to stand during a specific point in a lesson were purpose-driven.

Teacher Z was a nonexemplar. She was pleasantly marginal, but largely ineffective. It was impossible to identify a single positive, purpose-driven instructional move in her meanderings through a "lesson." Sometimes Teacher Z purposefully stopped "teaching" and assigned easy seatwork to her students while she shuffled papers at her desk—a clever ploy, she thought, to make me go away and leave her alone. Sometimes, Teacher Z actually attempted to teach a lesson, but unfortunately, it was usually unrelated to any of the outcomes or content of her grade level.

What Research Says About Instructional Moves

Figure 1.3 displays a set of research citations that demonstrate how the various instructional moves, either individually or together with other moves, positively impact student learning. Although you are not likely to track down all of these studies and reviews, they are included to demonstrate research support for this first category of literacy look-fors. Keep in mind that the citations in this figure and others in this chapter are illustrative rather than exhaustive.

Figure 1.3: Research Showing How Instructional Moves Impact Student Learning

Activating-Connecting	Afflerbach, 1990a, 1990b; Bransford, 1984; Brown, Smiley, Day, Townsend, & Lawton, 1977; Dole, Valencia, Greer, & Wardrop, 1991; Knapp, 1995; Neuman, 1988; Palincsar & Brown, 1984; Pearson, Roehler, Dole, & Duffy, 1992; Roberts, 1988; Tharp, 1982; Wood, Winne, & Pressley, 1989
Affirming-Appreciating	Aspy & Roebuck, 1977; Brophy, 1981; Pintrich & Schunk, 1996; Stipek, 1993
Annotating	Pressley, El-Dinary, & Brown, 1992
Assessing	Black, Harrison, Lee, Marshall, & Wiliam, 2003; Bursuck & Blanks, 2010; Fuchs et al., 2007
Attributing	Covington, 1984; Dweck, 1975; Howard, 1990, 1995; Howard & Hammond, 1985; Resnick, 1995, 1999; Weiner, 1972
Coaching-Facilitating	Collins, 1991; Collins et al., 1989; Mason, Roehler, & Duffy, 1984; Pearson & Gallagher, 1983; Pressley, Wharton, McDonald, Allington, et al., 2001; Pressley, El-Dinary, Gaskins, et al., 1992; Taylor, Brown, & Neuman, et al., 2000; Vygotsky, 1978
Constructing	Borkowski & Muthukrishna, 1992; Brown & Campione, 1994; Fielding & Pearson, 1994; Pressley, El-Dinary, & Brown, 1992; Pressley, El-Dinary, Gaskins, et al., 1992; Pressley et al., 1995

Differentiating	Connor, Morrison, Fishman, Schatschneider, & Underwood, 2007; Connor, Morrison, & Katch, 2004; Connor, Morrison, & Petrella, 2004; Connor, Schatschneider, Fishman, & Morrison, 2008; Lalley & Gentile, 2009; Willingham, 2005
Directly Instructing	Adams & Carnine, 2003; Brophy & Good, 1986; Bursuck & Blanks, 2010; Bursuck & Damer, 2010; Rosenshine, 1986; Rosenshine, 1997; Stockard & Engelmann, 2010
Explaining	Duffy, 2002; Duffy et al., 1987; Rosenshine, 1979
Giving Directions	Brophy & Good, 1986; Porter & Brophy, 1988
Grouping	Mosteller, Light, & Sachs, 1996; Vaughn, Hughes, Moody, & Elbaum, 2001
Guiding Practice	Good & Grouws, 1979; Hunter, 1982; Rosenshine, 1997; Willingham, 2004
Modeling	Afflerbach, 2002; Bereiter & Bird, 1985; Collins, Brown, & Holum, 1991; Davey, 1983; Herber & Herber, 1993; Pressley, El-Dinary, & Brown, et al., 1992; Wade, 1990
Motivating	Brophy, 1981, 1985, 1987; Bogner et al., 2002; Meichenbaum & Biemiller, 1998; Pressley, Raphael, Gallagher, & DiBella, 2004
Nurturing-Mentoring	Aspy & Roebuck, 1977; Noddings, 1984; Pintrich & Schunk, 1996
Questioning	Davey & McBride, 1986; King, 1989, 1990, 1992; King, Biggs, & Lipsky, 1984; Nolte & Singer, 1985; Rosenshine, Meister, & Chapman, 1996; Singer & Dolan, 1982; Smolkin & Donovan, 2000; Wong, Wong, Perry, & Sawatsky, 1986
Recapping	Carr & Ogle, 1987; Pressley, El-Dinary, Gaskins, et al., 1992
Redirecting	Saphier & Gower, 1997
Reminding	Pressley, El-Dinary, Gaskins, et al., 1992
Reteaching	Block, 1971; Block & Anderson, 1975; Bloom, 1971, 1974; Carroll, 1989; Gentile et al., 1982; Gentile & Lalley, 2003; Gentile, Voelkl, Mt. Pleasant, & Monaco, 1995; see The Scholar's Loop in Saphier & Gower, 1997, pp. 322–328
Scaffolding	Dickson, Collins, Simmons, & Kame'enui, 1998; Hogan & Pressley, 1997; Pressley et al., 2004; Rogoff, 1990; Vygotsky, 1978; Wood et al., 1976; Wood, Bruner, & Ross, 1976; Wood & Middleton, 1975

Teacher Exemplars and Nonexemplars for Instructional Moves

Recall an earlier statement in the introduction when we equated the terms *look-for* and *exemplar*. The descriptions of the look-fors are intended to serve as exemplars or models, both for you (the principal, as you look for that exemplar in the classrooms of your school), and for your teachers (once they begin to use the look-fors as the basis for their study and discussion in team meetings, and later to go on classroom walkthroughs as a team). A set of teacher exemplars and nonexemplars for each instructional move is shown in figure 1.4. In order to help you acquire a comfort level with each look-for, the descriptions in the teacher exemplar column repeat the look-for descriptions found in the observation protocol in figure 1.2 (page 15). Whenever you are uncertain about what you may be seeing in a classroom, refresh your memory by revisiting these opposite ends of an imagined effective instruction continuum.

Figure 1.4: Teacher Exemplars and Nonexemplars of Instructional Moves

Instructional Move	Teacher Exemplar	Teacher Nonexemplar
Activating-Connecting	The teacher generates interest in learning, activates prior knowledge, and connects instruction to the real world or to the solution of real problems.	The teacher does not tap into the experiences and background knowledge of her students. Lessons are presented as they are found in the teachers' manual with no observable modifications for the unique make-up of the class.
Affirming-Appreciating	The teacher appreciates, encourages, praises, or rewards students' actions, attitudes, thinking processes, verbal statements, and work products. The praise is specific and focuses on excellent work products as well as improvements in students' thinking and efforts.	The teacher is seldom observed praising or affirming students, and many teacher statements are negative, sarcastic, or punitive. The teacher often articulates the opinion to students that they need to develop their own internal motivations and should not expect compliments from him.
Annotating	The teacher adds additional information while reading a text with students or during a group discussion—information that students do not have, but need in order to make sense of the discussion or text. The teacher builds background and vocabulary knowledge as often as possible using relevant examples from students' experiences.	The teacher does not add information to that provided in the textbook, information that would enable struggling students to make connections to what is being taught. She simply assigns the story, leaving struggling students confused about what the text means.

Instructional Move	Teacher Exemplar	Teacher Nonexemplar
Assessing	The teacher determines both formally (through testing) and informally (through questioning) what students have learned and where instruction needs to be differentiated for all students to achieve mastery.	The teacher rarely uses informal assessments during instruction and uses formal assessments only to assign report card grades.
Attributing	The teacher communicates in specific ways to students that their accomplishments are the result of effort, wise decision making, attending to the task, and exercising good judgment and perseverance, rather than their intelligence or ability.	The teacher acts surprised when students do well and generally attributes their success to either their ability levels or to good luck.
Coaching-Facilitating	The teacher thinks along with students and helps them develop their own ideas, rather than directing their thinking and telling them what to do.	The teacher gives the right answers to students who ask questions so they can fill in the blank, turn in the worksheet, and get credit.
Constructing	The teacher and students work collaboratively to construct multiple meanings from conversations, discussions, and the reading of text.	The teacher does not work collaboratively with students to discuss the meaning of a story or article. He tells them his interpretation of the text.
Differentiating	The teacher calibrates the difficulty of learning tasks so as to create the best match possible with students' assessed skills and knowledge.	The teacher does not provide additional opportunities for learning to students who are struggling. Instruction is based on the textbook and moves at a pace suited to the most advanced students.
Directly Instructing	The teacher uses a direct, explicit, systematic, and supportive approach to teaching.	The teacher does not directly instruct students. All instruction is delivered in a whole-class setting and is designed for average students.
Explaining	The teacher tells students what will happen in a lesson, what the goal is, why it's being done, how it will help students, and what the roles of the teacher and students will be during the lesson.	Students seldom have an idea of the objective or purpose of a lesson. If asked by an observer what the lesson is about or what they are supposed to be learning, students are unable to respond.

continued →

Instructional Move	Teacher Exemplar	Teacher Nonexemplar
Giving Directions	The teacher gives clear and concise verbal instructions (supported by written directions, picture cues, or modeling as needed) that help students see how they are going to get from where they are at the beginning of a lesson, task, or unit to the completion of the task or outcome.	The teacher gives only verbal directions for assignments and activities. She does not ask students if they have questions, and she does not provide visual cues, more detail, or a repetition of the instructions for struggling students.
Grouping	The teacher uses benchmark assessment results to group and re-group students according to their specific academic needs for scaffolded instruction, enrichment, or specialized interventions.	The teacher uses only one kind of grouping arrangement: whole-group instruction. Students never have opportunities to work with a partner or complete a collaborative group project with classmates. The teacher does not form small groups to provide extended teaching or more practice for struggling students.
Guiding Practice	The teacher leads students through rehearsals of skills, processes, or routines to ensure understanding, accuracy, and automaticity.	The teacher does not provide extra practice during class time for struggling students. Instead, he sends worksheets to parents asking them to provide practice at home.
Modeling	The teacher thinks aloud regarding the cognitive processing of text and physically represents that thinking by constructing graphic organizers or writing in response to reading while students observe.	The teacher does not think aloud for students about her own reading comprehension, and she does not model how to construct organizers or write in response to reading. She gives assignments, collects work, and gives grades.
Motivating	The teacher encourages, inspires, and stimulates his students to achieve both personal and group goals by scaffolding instruction, affirming academic efforts, and providing extrinsic rewards as needed to jump-start struggling students.	The teacher uses teaching behaviors that undermine student motivation. Examples of this are competition rather than cooperation, public grading, very easy or boring tasks, giving negative feedback, and highlighting students' failures. Other examples include attributing students' successes and failures to luck, ability, or task difficulty, scapegoating students, and administering frequent reprimands.

Instructional Move	Teacher Exemplar	Teacher Nonexemplar
Nurturing-Mentoring	The teacher communicates positive expectations and a caring attitude, and takes a personal interest in the success of students.	The teacher uses teaching behaviors that communicate low expectations, apathy regarding the success of his students, and a distant attitude toward students.
Questioning	The teacher uses a variety of questioning techniques and types of questions to stimulate students' thinking, while also teaching students how to ask and answer their own questions.	The teacher uses one type of question, often questions to which she has a preconceived answer in mind. A small group of students in the classroom answer almost all of the questions that are asked.
Recapping	The teacher summarizes what has been concluded, learned, or constructed during a given lesson or discussion, tells students why this new learning is important, and lets them know where they can apply it in the future.	Lessons end abruptly with no closure, and the teacher rarely summarizes what was accomplished or learned.
Redirecting	The teacher monitors the level of student attention and engagement and uses a variety of techniques, prompts, and signals to regain or redirect students' attention to the learning task. The teacher is able to transition students from one activity to another with minimal time loss.	The teacher does not regularly pay attention to students who are off task. When he does, he has a limited repertoire of attention-getting signals, with most of them being negative in tone.
Reminding	The teacher causes students to remember or think more deeply about an idea or concept that has been previously taught, or restates something that has been previously taught in a novel way to ensure their remembering.	The teacher does not consider that students might need reminding and does not help students make connections between the learning of today and prior learning.
Reteaching	The teacher teaches recursively by repeatedly coming back to important skills, concepts, outcomes, or standards, giving students multiple opportunities to achieve mastery.	The teacher teaches a concept or skill, tests students, considers the concept taught, and moves on without regard for the students who have not achieved mastery.

continued →

Instructional Move	Teacher Exemplar	Teacher Nonexemplar
Scaffolding	The teacher supports students at their independent learning levels, enabling them to solve problems, carry out tasks, master content and skills, utilize appropriate cognitive strategies, and generally achieve goals that would otherwise be impossible for them.	The teacher consistently responds to students as though *they* are totally responsible for their own learning. He does not scaffold difficult material for struggling students and frequently says to students and colleagues, "Well, I had to get it on my own. Nobody ever explained it to me."

*Visit **go.solution-tree.com/literacy** to download and print this figure.*

Literacy Look-Fors: Teacher-Managed Instructional Activities

Teacher-managed instructional activities are lessons in which teachers provide targeted, direct, explicit, systematic, supportive instruction to students based on their assessed needs, for the various curricular components of a balanced literacy program. For these look-fors, the type of instruction remains constant (targeted, direct, explicit, systematic, and supportive) even as the curricular components (for example, literacy content) shift. In some classrooms, depending on the assessed needs of students, teachers may be teaching several teacher-managed lessons daily.

The look-fors in this category (figure 1.5) are aligned with the curricular components of literacy shown in the first column. This set of eight look-fors is sometimes challenging for administrators to pick out in classrooms. You must be aware of and sensitive to the multiple variables that impact teacher-managed instructional activities: (1) the current skill levels and learning strengths of students, (2) students' position on the grade-level mastery continuum (how far below or above grade level they are), and (3) the cognitive complexity and demands of the curricular component (such as discrete skills like phonemic awareness and word identification skills versus the higher-level thinking skills required for reading comprehension). In order to search out and identify teacher-managed instructional activities during classroom walkthroughs, you must be fully cognizant of the literacy curricula at every grade level, as well as the type and number of small groups being taught by teachers. The presence of well-designed and delivered teacher-managed instruction in classrooms at every grade level will enable your school to reach those struggling students who can all too easily fall through the cracks. As you begin to look for these exemplars in classrooms, you may discover that designing and delivering teacher-managed lessons for struggling students is a challenge for some teachers, especially novices. Many principals find that this category needs to be heavily supported with embedded professional development.

Figure 1.5: Look-Fors Observation Protocol—Teacher-Managed Instructional Activities

Curricular Component	Definition
Phonemic Awareness	As appropriate to the assessed needs of students, the teacher directly and explicitly teaches students how to blend sounds to make words and how to segment words into sounds.
Word Identification	As appropriate to the assessed needs of students, the teacher directly and explicitly teaches the alphabetic principle, sound-spelling correspondences, and the application of this knowledge to the decoding of unfamiliar words.
Spelling	As appropriate to the assessed needs of students, the teacher directly teaches the following linguistic skills needed for proficient reading and spelling: phonemic awareness, orthographic knowledge, morphological awareness, semantic knowledge, and mental orthographic images.
Fluency	As appropriate to the assessed needs of students, the teacher provides the type and amount of reading in accessible text students need in order to acquire the ability to read so effortlessly and automatically that working memory is available for the ultimate purpose of reading—extracting and constructing meaning from the text.
Vocabulary	As appropriate to the assessed needs of students, the teacher directly and explicitly teaches the pronunciations, spellings, and meanings of words students need to understand text.
Comprehension	As appropriate to the assessed needs of students, the teacher directly and explicitly teaches students how to extract and construct meaning from text using the seven cognitive strategies used by skilled readers and consistently models those strategies for students by thinking aloud about personal reading comprehension.
Reading a Lot	As appropriate to the assessed needs of students, the teacher directly and explicitly motivates students to become lifelong readers and learners.
Writing	As appropriate to the assessed needs of students, the teacher directly and explicitly teaches students how to write in response to reading or in the service of reading comprehension using various written formats such as graphic organizers, short answers, essays, and reports.

*Visit **go.solution-tree.com/literacy** to download and print this figure.*

The grade levels at which the various curricular components are generally taught are indicated by an X in the appropriate curricular column in figure 1.6. Note that when you are using a core program from a mainstream educational publisher, the difficulty level is geared toward students who are slightly below average, average, or slightly above average. Struggling students who are well below grade level or accelerated students who are well above grade level will require learning opportunities that are especially targeted to their assessed needs.

Figure 1.6: Curricular Components Across the Grades

Grade	PA	Phonics	Spelling	Fluency	Vocabulary	Comprehension	Reading a Lot	Writing
Pre-K	X				X	X	X	
K	X	X	X		X	X	X	X
1	X	X	X	X	X	X	X	X
2		X	X	X	X	X	X	X
3			X		X	X	X	X
4			X		X	X	X	X
5			X		X	X	X	X

Source: Adapted from McEwan (2009b).

The Big Idea of Teacher-Managed Instructional Activities

The big idea of teacher-managed instructional activities is that instruction is direct, explicit, and scaffolded. Teacher-managed instruction is never indirect (for example, implicit or unspoken) in nature. The teacher-managed literacy look-fors each have multiple dimensions and variables that interact with the needs of students at given points during the school year, thus necessitating the need for teachers to provide differing amounts and types of scaffolding for the various curricular components taught at that grade level. For example, at the beginning of kindergarten, a teacher-managed instructional activity (lesson) would be provided for a small group of students whose formative assessments show they are not meeting the grade-level benchmarks in phonemic awareness skills. The teacher carefully targets her instruction to the precise level of difficulty at which struggling students can experience success, and she provides enough guided practice so her students can achieve mastery.

Teachers can scaffold instruction in several ways, thus making this particular set of look-fors more challenging to see in classrooms and more difficult for teachers to execute. Teachers can vary the time they allocate for teaching or practicing certain key skills, vary the difficulty of the text they expect students to comprehend (either in terms of actual reading level or in the way it is orga-nized and presented) or vary the cognitive complexity of the tasks students are expected to perform on the text (such as summarizing the text versus answer-ing a factual recall question). Teachers can also vary the type of curriculum, providing a more specialized and intensive program.

What Research Says About Teacher-Managed Instructional Activities

Figure 1.7 provides citations to articles, research studies, and reviews of research showing the effectiveness of teacher-managed instructional activi-ties to raise students' literacy levels. Note that for each curricular component, the teacher provides instruction that is direct, explicit, and supportive. The teacher-managed instructional activities in the first column state the skills and strategies that are the primary focus of the curricular component that appears parenthetically at the end of the description. You may be surprised by the number of studies cited in this particular category. They are for the most part experimental and quasi-experimental studies in which various methodologies for instructing the most difficult-to-teach students were compared for their effectiveness in getting results with struggling students.

Figure 1.7: Research Showing How Teacher-Managed Instruction Impacts Student Learning

Teacher-Managed Instruction Curricular Component	Research Studies and Reviews
Explicit, systematic, supportive instruction in how to blend sounds to make words and how to segment words into sounds (phonemic awareness)	Ball & Blachman, 1991; Blachman, Ball, Black, & Tangel, 1994; Byrne & Fielding-Barnsley, 1989, 1993, 1995; Castle, Riach, & Nicholson, 1994; Cunningham, 1990; Frost & Peterson, 1988; Lie, 1991; Lundberg, O'Connor, Jenkins, & Slocum, 1993; Torgesen, Wagner, & Rashotte, 1997; Vellutino & Scanlon, 1987; Wagner et al., 1997; Wagner, Torgesen, & Rashotte, 1994
Explicit systematic, supportive instruction in word identification skills to include the alphabetic principle, sound-spelling relationships, and the application of this knowledge to the decoding of unfamiliar words (phonics)	Connor et al., 2007; Connor et al., 2008; Connor, Morrison, & Katch, 2004; Connor, Morrison, & Petrella, 2004; Connor, Morrison, & Slominski, 2006; Ehri, 1980, 1995, 1997a, 1997b, 1998; Just & Carpenter, 1987; Patterson & Coltheart, 1987; Rack, Hulme, Snowling, & Wightman, 1994; Rayner & Pollatsek, 1989; Reitsma, 1983; Share, 1999

continued →

Teacher-Managed Instruction Curricular Component	Research Studies and Reviews
Explicit systematic, supportive instruction in the linguistic skills needed for proficient reading and spelling (spelling)	Adams, 1990; Apel, 2007; Apel & Masterson, 2001; Apel, Masterson, & Niessen, 2004; Berninger et al., 2002; Ehri, 1997a; Kelman & Apel, 2004; Roberts & Meiring, 2006; Santoro, Coyne, & Simmons, 2006; Treiman, 1998; Treiman & Bourassa, 2000
Targeted provision of the type and amount of accessible text students need in order to acquire fluency (fluency)	Allington, 1980; Hiebert & Fisher, 2005, 2006; Kuhn & Stahl, 2003; McGill-Franzen & McDermott, 1978; O'Connor, Swanson, & Geraghty, 2010; Pikulski & Chard, 2005; Stahl & Heubach, 2005; Torgesen & Hudson, 2006
Explicit, systematic, supportive instruction in the pronunciation, spelling, and meaning of words students need in order to understand text (vocabulary)	Beck, McKeown, & Kucan, 2002; Dickinson & Tabors, 2001; Graves, Juel, & Graves, 2004; Hiebert, 2008b; Johnson, Johnson, & Schlicting, 2004; Pearson, Cervetti, Bravo, Hiebert, & Arya, 2005; Stahl, 1999
Explicit, systematic, supportive instruction in the seven cognitive strategies of highly skilled readers (comprehension)	National Institute of Child Health and Human Development, 2000; Pressley et al., 1995; Snow, 2002; Trabasso & Bouchard, 2000, 2002; Wood, Woloshyn, & Willoughby, 1995
Explicit, systematic, supportive instruction in how to write in response to reading and in the service of reading comprehension using various written formats such as summaries, short answers, essays, and reports (writing)	Berninger et al., 2002; Collins, 1998; Collins, Lee, et al., 2008; Fitzgerald & Shanahan, 2000; Graham & Perin, 2007

Teacher Exemplars and Nonexemplars of Teacher-Managed Instructional Activities

Figure 1.8 contains teacher exemplars and nonexemplars of teacher-managed instructional activities to help you discern the critical attributes of each look-for as well as hone your ability to distinguish between best practices that get results and less effective instructional approaches. The exemplars and nonexemplars in this category differ from those in the instructional moves category. The exemplars and nonexemplars of instructional moves are generally polar opposites or points on the far ends of an effectiveness continuum. However, teacher-managed instructional activities are designed based on the assessed needs of students—that is, they are targeted. In the teacher exemplar and nonexemplar for phonemic awareness, for example, the assumption is that the students being taught have phonemic deficiencies. Students who

have strong phonemic skills would likely not need explicit phonemic awareness instruction. The big idea of teacher-managed instructional activities is
that these activities, lessons, or interventions will always be targeted to the
assessed needs of students. The nonexemplars in figure 1.8 describe practices
that might be acceptable when teaching average and above-average students.
Those nonexemplars are missing the mark because teachers have selected
practices that are not recommended for struggling students. The effectiveness of teacher-managed instruction depends on teachers' accurate knowledge
about the following three variables: (1) the current skill levels and learning
strengths of their students, (2) students' positions on the grade-level mastery
continuum (how far below or above grade level they are), and (3) the cognitive complexity and demands of the curricular component (discrete skills like
phonemic awareness and word identification skills versus higher-level thinking skills required for reading comprehension). The assessed needs of an individual student or small group of students dictate which instructional activities
are used and in what types of settings (whole group, small group, or individual) those activities are best taught.

Figure 1.8: Teacher Exemplars and Nonexemplars of Teacher-Managed Instructional Activities

Curricular Component	Teacher Exemplar	Teacher Nonexemplar
Teacher-Managed Phonemic Awareness Instruction	As appropriate to the assessed needs of students, the teacher directly and explicitly teaches students how to blend sounds to make words and how to segment words into sounds.	The teacher models the individual sounds for students and says the word fast, but does not provide opportunities for struggling students to say the sounds and say the word fast in unison enough times over a period of days to master blending sounds to make words.
Teacher-Managed Word Identification Instruction	As appropriate to the assessed needs of students, the teacher directly and explicitly teaches the alphabetic principle, sound-spelling correspondences, and the application of this knowledge to the decoding of unfamiliar words.	During the reading of the story, the teacher suggests that a student get the first or second letter(s) started and then guess at what the word is. Struggling students become confused and adopt a guessing habit, which will lead to fluency and comprehension problems at the next reading level, if not sooner.

continued →

Curricular Component	Teacher Exemplar	Teacher Nonexemplar
Teacher-Managed Spelling Instruction	As appropriate to the assessed needs of students, the teacher directly teaches the following linguistic skills needed for proficient reading and spelling: phonemic awareness, orthographic knowledge, morphological awareness, semantic knowledge, and mental orthographic images.	The teacher randomly selects dissimilar words that have not been analyzed for their various linguistic properties, thereby setting struggling students up for failure.
Teacher-Managed Fluency Instruction	As appropriate to the assessed needs of students, the teacher directly teaches the following linguistic skills needed for proficient reading and spelling: phonemic awareness, orthographic knowledge, morphological awareness, semantic knowledge, and mental orthographic images.	The teacher expects students to read books that are too difficult, resulting in dysfluent reading full of errors. The teacher constantly interrupts students to correct those mistakes, and the students' reading becomes more tentative. Oral reading becomes a word-by-word reading performance that does not contribute to fluency.
Teacher-Managed Vocabulary Instruction	As appropriate to the assessed needs of students, the teacher directly teaches the pronunciations, spellings, and meanings of words students need to understand text.	The teacher regularly expects students to look up the definitions of new words in the dictionary and write sentences. She does not supply student-friendly definitions or give students a scaffolded approach to writing the sentences.
Teacher-Managed Comprehension Instruction	As appropriate to the assessed needs of students, the teacher directly teaches students how to extract and construct meaning from text using the seven cognitive strategies used by skilled readers, and consistently models those strategies for students by thinking aloud about personal reading comprehension.	The teacher assigns short paragraphs to be read, each with three to four questions. Students complete the assignment independently, and trade and grade each other's worksheets. The teacher takes the grades orally for her gradebook.
Teacher-Managed Reading a Lot Instruction	As appropriate to the assessed needs of students, the teacher directly motivates students to become lifelong readers and learners.	The teacher communicates verbally to both students and colleagues that it is not his job to manage students' independent reading. He relies on parents, the school librarian, and Accelerated Reader to motivate reading.

Curricular Component	Teacher Exemplar	Teacher Nonexemplar
Teacher-Managed Writing Instruction	As appropriate to the assessed needs of students, the teacher directly teaches students how to write in response to reading, or in the service of reading comprehension using various written formats (such as drawings, graphic organizers, short answers, essays, and reports).	The teacher has students writing their own books based on a predictable book (a book that repeats one set of words on each new page) as a group activity. They copy the words she has chosen for them on their papers.

*Visit **go.solution-tree.com/literacy** to download and print this figure.*

Literacy Look-Fors: Components of Teacher With-It-Ness

Teacher with-it-ness is the state of being on top of, tuned in to, aware of, and in complete control of the various organizational and management facets of classroom life. With-it-ness also includes the ability to preview, project, and predict the challenges and contingencies of an upcoming school year combined with the expertise to proactively design a set of expectations (routines, rubrics, and rules) that, when directly and explicitly taught during the first three weeks of school, will prepare students for the rigors of mastering or exceeding the prescribed grade-level literacy outcomes.

Jacob Kounin coined the term *with-it-ness* in 1977 and defined it as a teacher's sense of omniscience about what is happening in the classroom combined with the ability to multitask and shift gears during instruction to deal with whatever contingencies arise. Note that the definition of *with-it-ness* on which this chapter is based encompasses a broader range of literacy look-fors than Kounin's original definition.

The first sentence of the with-it-ness definition on which this category of look-fors is based was developed during the writing of *10 Traits of Highly Effective Teachers* (McEwan, 2003). I concluded after interviews with teachers, parents, administrators, and students, and a review of the effective instruction literature that with-it-ness was definitely one of the ten traits. While working on a qualitative study of more than ninety teachers selected by their principals as exemplars of with-it-ness, I subsequently broadened my definition to include teaching the 3Rs (routines, rubrics, and rules) during the first three weeks of the school year (McEwan, 2006). Figure 1.9 (page 32) defines the look-fors in the teacher with-it-ness category.

Figure 1.9: Look-Fors Observation Protocol—Components of Teacher With-It-Ness

Climate Management	The teacher creates a positive and productive classroom environment in which all students achieve to their maximum potential.
Lesson Planning	The teacher designs well-organized lessons using the elements of lesson design that are appropriate to the content and differentiated as appropriate to students' needs.
Lesson Presentation	The teacher uses effective communication skills, organizes an appropriate number and variety of instructional activities, and selects appropriate instructional moves and presentation techniques.
Lesson Management	The teacher regularly checks for understanding during lessons and makes mid-course corrections to instruction (fine-tuning content, difficulty, or pace) to ensure that students can understand.
Time Management	The teacher uses allocated learning time productively, thereby maximizing academic learning time for all students and interactive learning time for students at risk.
Student Engagement	The teacher productively engages students in teacher-directed lessons, facilitates cooperative work with other students, and provides appropriate levels of student-managed learning activities thereby ensuring that all students achieve to their maximum levels.
Student Management	The teacher handles conflict and confrontation with authority, calmness, and confidence and is able to prevent, forestall, anticipate, and disarm behavioral problems with students.
Organizational Routines	The teacher designs, teaches, and implements a variety of organizational routines to facilitate the movement of students, the flow of paper and instructional materials, and the adherence to schedules.
Academic Routines	The teacher designs, teaches, and implements a variety of academic routines that facilitate and motivate high levels of literacy learning.
Social Routines	The teacher designs, teaches, and implements a variety of social routines to ensure positive and productive interpersonal communications and relationships between students.
Rules	The teacher designs, teaches, and implements a set of principles to guide students' behavior and attitudes.
Rubrics	The teacher designs, teaches, and implements a variety of performance-based assessment tools (rubrics, checklists, or rating scales) to communicate behavioral, social, and academic expectations to students.

*Visit **go.solution-tree.com/literacy** to download and print this figure.*

The Big Idea of Teacher With-It-Ness

Many teachers think of content as their first priority when planning for instruction, but I discovered when writing *How to Survive and Thrive in the First Three Weeks of School* (2006) that the most effective teachers use the first few weeks of the school year to lay a solid management foundation in their classrooms. This is the big idea of teacher with-it-ness: *being at least a dozen steps ahead of your students every minute of every day*. Effective teachers have a game plan to maximize their students' academic success during the full thirty-six weeks of the school year. With-it teachers are proactive pedagogues who know precisely how they want their students to "play" the academic game. Once taught, practiced, and mastered, the routines, rules, and rubrics result in classrooms that are positive, productive, well organized, and focused.

The biggest mistake many teachers make—both brand-new *and* experienced ones—is to launch into skills or content instruction without first teaching the 3Rs. They erroneously assume that their students will understand their directions the first time they are given and know how to read their minds thereafter. With-it teachers explicitly model and explain the essential routines, rubrics, and rules students are expected to follow.

What Research Says About Teacher With-It-Ness

In contrast to the experimental and quasi-experimental research that supported the category of teacher-managed instructional activities, we have only correlational research to show the effects of teacher with-it-ness on student learning (see figure 1.10). However, most of the citations shown are meta-analyses (reviews) of research in which a large number of studies are statistically combined to produce an average effect size. The sheer number and effects of the correlational studies make up for the fact that they are not experimental. Figure 1.10 summarizes the studies showing the power of the various components of teacher with-it-ness to positively impact student literacy levels. Note that the with-it-ness components are grouped into larger, more inclusive categories reflecting the nature of the studies.

Figure 1.10: Research Showing How Teacher With-It-Ness Impacts Student Learning

With-It-Ness Component	Research Studies and Reviews
Climate Management and Social Routines	Aspy & Roebuck, 1977; Brophy, 1999; Bryk & Schneider, 2002; Cabello & Terrell, 1993; Glasser, 1969
Designing and Delivering Literacy Instruction	Foorman, 2007; Foorman et al., 2006; Foorman & Torgesen, 2001; Pressley, Wharton-McDonald, & Mistretta, 1998; Rosenshine, 1971, 1986, 1997

continued →

With-It-Ness Component	Research Studies and Reviews
Time Management During Literacy Instruction	Anderson, 1975; Bloom, 1974; Fisher, 1978; Fisher & Berliner, 1985; Rosenshine, 1981; Rosenshine & Berliner, 1978; Stallings, 1980
Student Engagement and Motivation During Literacy Instruction	Bogner et al., 2002; Dolezal, Welsh, Pressley, & Vincent, 2003; Gambrell, 1996; Gunther, Reffel, Barnett, Lee, & Patrick, 2004; Haydon, Mancil, & Van Loan, 2009; Heward, 1994; Heward et al., 1996; Randolph, 2007
Student Management	Evertson, 1989; Evertson, Emmer, Clements, & Worsham, 1994; Marzano, Marzano, & Pickering, 2003; Saphier & Gower, 1997
Classroom Management and Organization	Anderson, Evertson, & Emmer, 1979; Emmer, Evertson, & Anderson, 1979, 1980; Evertson, 1989; Wang, Haertel, & Walberg, 1993
Proactive Instruction of Organizational Routines, Academic Routines, Social Routines, Rules, and Rubric During the First Three Weeks of the School Year	Emmer et al., 1979, 1980; Kounin, 1977

Exemplars and Nonexemplars of Teacher With-It-Ness

Figure 1.11 provides descriptions of exemplars and nonexemplars of teacher with–it–ness. These look-fors are easy to overlook during classroom walk-throughs because they function behind the scenes in classrooms of highly effective teachers. However, the minute you enter a classroom *without* a with-it teacher in charge, the disorganization, wasted time, and in some cases, complete chaos will get your attention immediately.

Literacy Look-Fors: Student-Managed Learning Activities

Student-managed learning activities are tasks, assignments, or projects for which students have acquired the necessary skills and strategies to apply them successfully at their independent reading levels. This particular category of literacy look-fors does not fit neatly into the template we have used for describing earlier categories.

Figure 1.11: Teacher Exemplars and Nonexemplars of With-It-Ness

With-It-Ness Component	Teacher With-It-Ness Exemplar	Teacher With-It-Ness Nonexemplar
Climate Management	The teacher creates a positive and productive classroom environment in which all students achieve to their maximum potential.	The teacher rarely makes positive and affirming statements and seldom smiles or speaks in a personal way to students. Students are rude to each other as well as to the teacher, and low achievement is the norm.
Lesson Planning (Designing)	The teacher designs well-organized lessons using the elements of lesson design that are appropriate to the content and differentiated as appropriate to students' needs.	The teacher seldom has a written plan for a lesson. Her lesson plan book is filled with page numbers of various textbooks, rather than learning objectives that students need to master as a result of her lessons.
Lesson Presentation (Delivery)	The teacher uses effective communication skills, organizes an appropriate number and variety of instructional activities, and selects appropriate instructional moves and presentation techniques.	The teacher has difficulty delivering a lesson with a beginning, middle, and conclusion. The teacher frequently injects sidebars and off-topic comments into the lesson that distract both him and his students.
Lesson Management	The teacher regularly checks for understanding during lessons and makes mid-course corrections to instruction (fine-tuning content, difficulty, or pace) to ensure that students can understand.	The teacher is unable to attend to more than one stimulus at a time and is unable to make adjustments to the lesson pace or difficulty during the lesson. The teacher frequently loses the attention of the entire class and is seldom able to re-engage students in a positive way.
Time Management	The teacher uses allocated learning time productively, thereby maximizing academic learning time for all students and interactive learning time for students at risk.	The teacher wastes a great deal of time talking about things that are unrelated to lesson objectives, and students are frequently engaged in inappropriate behavior while the teacher is talking. There is no evidence of organizational routines or timesavers.

continued →

With-It-Ness Component	Teacher With-It-Ness Exemplar	Teacher With-It-Ness Nonexemplar
Student Engagement	The teacher productively engages students in teacher-directed lessons, facilitates cooperative work with other students, and provides appropriate levels of student-managed learning activities, thereby ensuring that all students achieve to their maximum levels.	The teacher seems unaware of the large amount of wasted time in her classroom, during which no active instruction is occurring. Either students are not engaged in any type of student-managed learning activity, have not been given directions to begin an activity, are waiting for another task, or are not being supervised.
Student Management	The teacher handles conflict and confrontation with authority, calmness, and confidence. The teacher is able to prevent, forestall, anticipate, and disarm behavioral problems with students.	The teacher makes many negative statements, including comments that reflect her dislike of certain students. Students are often confused about what they should be doing and how they should be doing it, indicating that behavioral expectations have not been taught to them.
Organizational Routines	The teacher designs, teaches, and implements a variety of organizational routines to facilitate the movement of students, the flow of paper and instructional materials, and the adherence to schedules.	There are no apparent routines for students during transition times, beginning of the day, or ending of the day. Students appear disorganized and are often asking questions of one another such as, "What do we do now?"
Academic Routines	The teacher designs, teaches, and implements a variety of academic routines that facilitate and motivate high levels of literacy learning.	The teacher makes attempts to engage students in cooperative work, but has never explicitly taught them the social or organizational routines that would help cooperative work go smoothly. Students are talking at the same time, or one individual has taken over the group and is not letting other students have a turn.
Social Routines	The teacher designs, teaches, and implements a variety of social routines to ensure positive and productive interpersonal communication and relationships between students.	Student behavior does not give evidence that they have been taught specific social routines. Observed class discussions often degenerate into shouting and hand waving to get the teacher's attention.

With-It-Ness Component	Teacher With-It-Ness Exemplar	Teacher With-It-Ness Nonexemplar
Rules	The teacher designs, teaches, and implements a set of principles to guide students' behavior and attitudes.	There are no behavioral expectations or rubrics posted in the classroom, and the teacher seldom reminds students or refers them to principles or values that should guide their behavior and attitudes.
Rubrics	The teacher designs, teaches, and implements a variety of performance-based assessment tools (rubrics, checklists, or rating scales) to communicate behavioral, social, and academic expectations to students.	There are no posted rubrics for student behavior or work products. The grades on displayed student work exhibit a haphazard evaluation system.

Visit **go.solution-tree.com/literacy** *to download and print this figure.*

Earlier in the chapter, we introduced the concept of teacher-managed instructional activities and the importance of directly instructing students who are in the acquisition phase of literacy learning and then scaffolding the activities as students practice and consolidate those skills and strategies. In this category of look-fors, we turn the spotlight on the teacher's gradual release of responsibility to students for the successful application of those skills and strategies.

Figure 1.12 contains the literacy look-fors for student-managed learning activities. Note that in addition to the eight curricular components that parallel those found in the teacher-managed instructional activities (figure 1.6, page 26), there are two noncurricular components: self-management skills and metacognitive skills related to learning.

Figure 1.12: Look-Fors Observation Protocol—Student-Managed Learning Activities

Word Identification	As appropriate to their assessed independent reading levels, students are able to successfully apply phonemic decoding skills to identify new words.
Spelling	As appropriate to their assessed independent reading levels, students are able to successfully apply phonemic awareness skills, orthographic knowledge, and morphological awareness to correctly spell words.

continued →

Fluency	As appropriate to their assessed independent reading levels, students are able to read with fluency so that working memory is available for the ultimate purpose of reading—extracting and constructing meaning from the text.
Vocabulary	As appropriate to their assessed independent reading levels, students are able to successfully acquire and use new words that are directly taught as well as use context clues and other strategies to determine the meaning of new words in text.
Reading Comprehension	As appropriate to their assessed independent reading levels, students are able to successfully apply appropriate cognitive strategies to extract and construct meaning from text.
Reading a Lot	As appropriate to their assessed independent reading levels, students are able to engage in mindful silent reading of a large volume of text both in and out of school, at gradually increasing levels of difficulty, with personalized accountability.
Writing	As appropriate to their assessed independent reading levels, students are able to write in response to reading in various formats such as graphic organizers, short answers, essays, and reports.
Self-Management Skills	As appropriate to their assessed skills and strategy knowledge, students are able to exhibit the traits of highly successful students: responsibility, perseverance, dependability, diligence, motivation, orderliness, self-control, punctuality, attentiveness, and enthusiasm.
Metacognition About Learning	As appropriate to their assessed skills and strategy knowledge, students are able to think about their own learning in the context of these six learning concepts: read, reduce, organize, process, connect, and reflect.

*Visit **go.solution-tree.com/literacy** to download and print this figure.*

The Big Idea of Student-Managed Learning Activities

The big idea of student-managed learning activities is that some students in almost every grade level will not need the kind of direct and explicit instruction that the struggling students (described in the context of teacher-managed instructional activities) required. In fact, some students may not even need the whole-group instruction provided for average-achieving students. The students who are the topic of this category of look-fors are quite capable of managing their own learning with some *targeted* instruction that meets *their* specific assessed needs for more challenging assignments and accelerated learning. For example, kindergarten students who are already reading at a second-grade level will likely never require direct instruction in phonemic awareness skills. They need student-managed learning activities—opportunities to apply the skills and strategies they have already mastered in a variety of more challenging literacy learning activities.

What Research Says About Student-Managed Learning Activities

The research on student-managed learning (found in figure 1.13) is focused on accelerated students, students who have the content and skills in a specific curricular area to work independently while being supported with further instruction in self-management skills and metacognitive skills as they relate to students' understanding of how they learn. We know from two powerful studies (Connor, Morrison, & Katch, 2004; Connor, Morrison, & Petrella, 2004) that when students who are capable of managing their own learning activities in the classroom are held back and forced to move in tandem with a large group that is progressing more slowly, they do not achieve to the same levels as their counterparts whose teachers have released the responsibility for specific kinds of learning to them. This does not mean that the teacher does not work with these students. It simply means that these students are capable of applying skills and strategies without having direct instruction from the teacher.

Figure 1.13: Research Showing How Student-Managed Learning Activities Impact Student Learning

Word Identification	Connor, Morrison, & Katch, 2004; Connor et al., 2008
Spelling	Bosman & Van Ordern, 1997
Fluency	Stahl & Heubach, 2005
Vocabulary	Beck, McKeown, & Kucan, 2002; Hirsch, 2003; Pearson, 2006; Stahl, 2005
Reading Comprehension	Connor, Morrison, & Petrella, 2004; Pearson et al., 1992; Pressley et al., 1995
Reading a Lot	Carlson & Brosnahan, 2009; Pearson et al., 2005; Pearson, 2006
Writing	Bereiter & Scardamalia, 1987; Fitzgerald & Shanahan, 2000; Graham & Perrin, 2007
Self-Management Skills	Gaskins, 1980, 1994, 2005; Joseph & Konrad, 2009
Metacognition About Learning	Bereiter, 2002; Bransford, Brown, & Cocking, 2000; Caine & Caine, 1994; Craik & Tulving, 1975; Greeno, Collins, & Resnick, 1996; Joyce & Weil, 2008; Lambert & McCombs, 1998; Silverman & Casazza, 2000; Zimmerman, 1990, 1998, 2001; Zimmerman & Campillo, 2003; Zimmerman & Schunk, 2001

Exemplars and Nonexemplars of Student-Managed Learning Activities

Figure 1.14 contains exemplars and nonexemplars for student-managed learning activities. In classrooms where enriched and accelerated learning is systematically available to students, teachers find that many average and slightly above-average students respond to raised expectations and are willing to take on more responsibility for learning than had been granted to them by their teachers.

Figure 1.14: Exemplars and Nonexemplars of Student-Managed Learning Activities

Curricular Component	Exemplars of Student-Managed Learning Activity	Nonexemplars of Student-Managed Learning Activity
Word Identification	As appropriate to their assessed independent reading levels, students are able to successfully apply phonemic decoding skills to identify new words.	Students are expected to attend to instruction and complete work products at levels far below their assessed independent achievement levels.
Spelling	As appropriate to their assessed independent reading levels, students are able to successfully apply phonemic awareness skills, orthographic knowledge, and morphological awareness to correctly spell words.	Students are not accelerated to more challenging levels of word study to increase their knowledge of higher-level spelling skills in areas like morphology.
Fluency	As appropriate to their assessed independent reading levels, students are able to read with fluency so that working memory is available for the ultimate purpose of reading—extracting and constructing meaning from the text.	Students are expected to read and discuss text that is far below their actual assessed reading level.
Vocabulary	As appropriate to their assessed independent reading levels, students are able to successfully acquire and use new words that are directly taught, as well as use context clues and other strategies to determine the meaning of new words in text.	Students are not challenged by the type and amount of advanced vocabulary of which they are capable of mastering.

Curricular Component	Exemplars of Student-Managed Learning Activity	Nonexemplars of Student-Managed Learning Activity
Reading Comprehension	As appropriate to their assessed independent reading levels, students are able to successfully apply appropriate cognitive strategies to extract and construct meaning from text.	Students are not challenged to extract and construct meaning from more difficult texts in a small-group setting.
Reading a Lot	As appropriate to their assessed independent reading levels, students are able to engage in mindful silent reading of a large volume of text, both in and out of school, at gradually increasing levels of difficulty, with personalized accountability.	Students are reprimanded by the teacher for the amount and kind of reading they do in class, especially when this reading is done during instruction that is well below the students' ability level.
Writing	As appropriate to their assessed independent reading levels, students are able to write in response to reading in various formats (such as graphic organizers, short answers, essays, and reports).	Students are not expected to write to a higher standard and often slip into careless thinking and writing habits, thereby depressing their achievement.
Self-Management Skills	As appropriate to grade levels, students are able to exhibit the traits of highly successful students: responsibility, perseverance, dependability, diligence, motivation, orderliness, self-control, punctuality, attentiveness, and enthusiasm.	Students frequently develop nonexamples of these character traits when their academic needs are ignored.
Metacognition About Learning	As appropriate to grade levels, students are able to think about their own learning in the context of these six learning concepts: read, reduce, organize, process, connect, and reflect.	Students are not taught how to think about their own learning and consequently do not develop strategies to employ when work eventually becomes more difficult in advanced high school and college courses.

*Visit **go.solution-tree.com/literacy** to download and print this figure.*

Literacy Look-Fors: Classroom Artifacts

I have done classroom walkthroughs in schools all over the country and never cease to be amazed at the creativity and variety of artifacts teachers bring to and construct in their classrooms. The term *artifact* is one I've borrowed from archaeology: *an object made by a human being that has cultural or historical significance* (McKean, 2005). In an educational context, an artifact is also something that is made by a human being—a teacher, a student, or a group of students—that has educational significance. Figure 1.15 lists the set of literacy look-for artifacts that, when examined in the context of teaching and learning in a given classroom, can provide evidence of effective literacy instruction.

The classroom artifacts category excludes all manufactured items purchased at education stores. I will make exceptions for borders, backgrounds, letters, reading charts from core reading programs, and other artifacts that specifically support a required curriculum. In the classrooms of highly effective teachers, the walls and bulletin boards and even the windows are outcome-focused and learning-centered.

Figure 1.15: Look-Fors Observation Protocol—Classroom Artifacts

Classroom Libraries	The classroom contains a variety of books at various levels so all students can find accessible text to read independently.
Student Vocabulary Notebook	The vocabulary notebook contains a collection of the new words students have acquired during literacy instruction, words they have encountered in their own independent reading, and words the teacher has taught indirectly in the classroom.
Student Reading Log	The reading log contains a brief entry for each book a student has read independently outside of school or in the classroom. The log contains the title, author, and a one- or two-sentence summary about the book (a statement of the moral of the story or the main idea).
Posters and Chats	Charts containing steps or prompts to scaffold students' decoding of cognitive strategies are displayed where students can easily see them.
Student Literacy Centers	Student literacy centers are clearly labeled and furnished with organized materials that are accessible to students.
Content Standards or Lesson Objectives	As appropriate to the grade level, the content standard or lesson objective is stated in student-friendly language.
Exemplary Student Work	Exemplary student work is displayed on the walls and boards both inside and outside the classroom.
Word Wall	As appropriate to the grade level, important academic and content words are displayed on a word wall.
Graphic Organizers	Graphic organizers to summarize stories, articles, important concepts, or academic vocabulary are displayed and frequently used as examples by the teacher.

*Visit **go.solution-tree.com/literacy** to download and print this figure.*

The Big Idea of Classroom Artifacts

If administrators and teachers can get beyond the battle of the bulletin boards to understand that it's not what's on the bulletin boards per se that results in high levels of literacy learning, classroom observers can then examine classroom artifacts as evidence of solid teaching and learning and not merely a response to a mandate. There is a reason that artifacts are the last chapter in the book and not the first. Many of the artifacts are easy to create in the absence of teaching and learning. Those are the artifacts that money can buy at the teachers' store. Excellent teaching and long-lasting learning are priceless. Keep in mind when you are evaluating an artifact during a classroom observation: "It's usually the process that created the product that impacted student learning." Classroom artifacts are like vacation snapshots or videos. If you spend too much time taking pictures, you'll miss the point of being there.

What Research Says About Classroom Artifacts

Given today's standards-based focus, teachers are feeling the pressure to create classroom walls that support instruction and enhance learning. Principals are encouraged to "walk the walls" of their schools looking for evidence of learning objectives, procedure steps, whole-class brainstorming efforts, cooperative group work with multiple names attached to a work product, and student work centers in which something from every student is displayed (Downey, Steffy, English, Frase, & Poston, 2004). Figure 1.16 presents articles, books, and some research showing how various classroom artifacts, as used by effective teachers, impact student learning. Be careful not to fall into the trap of thinking, however, that any of these artifacts in and of themselves have the power to impact student learning. They must be mediated or acted on by a highly effective teacher. In some cases, a classroom artifact does not have a coherent body of research that has put it under the microscope and examined its impact on student learning apart from a myriad of other variables. So, be judicious in your use of figure 1.16.

Figure 1.16: Research Showing How Classroom Artifacts Impact Student Learning

Classroom Libraries	Brenner, Tompkins, Hiebert, Riley, & Miles, 2007
Student Vocabulary Notebook	Schmitt & Schmitt, 1995

continued →

Student Reading Log	Anderson, Wilson, & Fielding, 1988
Posters and Charts	Dickson et al., 1998
Student Literacy Centers	Florida Center for Reading Research, 2001
Content Standards or Instructional Objectives	Ainsworth, 2003; Duffy, Roehler, & Rackliffe, 1986; Marzano, 2009a
Exemplary Student Work	Reeves, 2010; Wiggins, 1991
Word Wall	Marzano, 2009c
Graphic Organizers	Hyerle, 1996; Hyerle, 2004; Proly, Rivers, & Schwartz, 2009

Exemplars and Nonexemplars of Classroom Artifacts

Figure 1.17 describes exemplars and nonexemplars of classroom artifacts. As you consider the nonexemplar, recall that classroom artifacts can be physical objects in the classroom, teacher-produced written documents, and student-produced work. Literacy look-for classroom artifacts are not manufactured for the mass market. They contribute to teaching and learning in individual classrooms.

Figure 1.17: Exemplars and Nonexemplars of Classroom Artifacts

Classroom Artifact	Classroom Artifact Exemplar	Classroom Artifact Nonexemplar
Classroom Libraries	The classroom contains a variety of books at various levels so all students can find accessible text to read independently.	The classroom library does not support the range of independent reading levels found in the students of the class.
Student Vocabulary Notebook	The vocabulary notebook contains a collection of the new words students have acquired during literacy instruction, words they have encountered in their own independent reading, and words the teacher has taught indirectly in the classroom.	Students are not expected or even encouraged to maintain a vocabulary notebook, thus decreasing the likelihood that they will experience the number of encounters with a new word that is needed for mastery.

Classroom Artifact	Classroom Artifact Exemplar	Classroom Artifact Nonexemplar
Student Reading Log	The reading log contains a brief entry for each book a student has read independently in the classroom. The log contains the title, author, and a one- or two-sentence summary of the book, a statement of the moral of the story, or the main idea.	Students do not maintain any record of their reading either in or out of the classroom. Hence, the teacher has no data to inform her decisions regarding the amount students are reading.
Posters and Charts	Charts containing steps or prompts to scaffold students' decoding of big words or use of cognitive strategies are displayed where students can easily see them and consult them when working on assignments.	There are no posters in the classroom in support of specific standards or outcomes. If there are posters, they have been purchased and seem not to be related to the curricula, but rather serve as decoration.
Student Literacy Centers	Student literacy centers are clearly labeled and furnished with organized materials that are easily accessible to students.	All instruction is whole group, regardless of the grade level, and there are no student literacy centers where students can learn to self-manage their reading and writing at their independent reading levels.
Content Standards or Lesson Objectives	As appropriate to the grade level, the content standard or lesson objective is stated in student-friendly language.	Content standards and objectives have been copied from a binder and have not been translated into student-friendly language.
Exemplary Student Work	Exemplary student work is displayed on the walls and boards both inside and outside the classroom.	There is a great deal of student work that is suspect in terms of its production by students (as opposed to parents).
Word Wall	As appropriate to the grade level, important academic and content words are displayed on a word wall.	When questioned, students appear not to know what the word wall is, why it is there, and what function it serves in their classroom.
Graphic Organizers	Graphic organizers to summarize stories, articles, important concepts, or academic vocabulary are displayed and frequently used as examples by the teacher.	If there are graphic organizers posted in the classroom, they were not created by students in conjunction with reading for meaning or organizing to study for a test.

*Visit **go.solution-tree.com/literacy** to download and print this figure.*

The Next Step

You have completed the first step to an effective implementation of literacy look-fors and classroom walkthroughs. Before you drift off to sleep tonight or while you are waiting for the subway or caught in a traffic jam, mentally enumerate the five categories of look-fors and summarize their big ideas. Next, we will tackle the topic of classroom walkthroughs.

Chapter 2

Understand the Classroom Walkthroughs

Rather than being seen solely as a vehicle to provide teachers with feedback, walkthroughs should be viewed as a vehicle for the observers to learn how strategies manifest themselves in the classroom.

—Marzano (2009b, p. 36)

1. Understand the literacy look-fors.

2. **Understand the classroom walkthroughs.**

3. Assess your instructional leadership capacity.

4. Orient your faculty to the look-fors and walkthroughs.

5. Collect and analyze look-for frequency data.

6. Develop, implement, and assess embedded professional development.

7. Use team walkthroughs to build school capacity.

Despite the belief of some that the mere presence of a principal in a classroom automatically improves instruction (which thereby raises achievement), classroom walkthroughs are not necessarily magical. In actuality, classroom walkthroughs are a source of some frustration and even a little guilt for some administrators.

In preparation for writing this book, I queried a random sample of principals in my database about their walkthrough procedures. Many were conducting classroom walkthroughs because they felt an obligation to do so. Some of them expressed anxiety and even embarrassment because their walkthroughs were haphazard and unfocused. Others felt guilty because they were not getting to all of their classrooms every day. In some instances, principals were only inspecting the classroom for the presence of a district-mandated artifact or practice so they could fill out a form to be inspected by the superintendent. Feedback to teachers ranged from a formal meeting to reflect on instruction to a fast-food coupon in the teacher's mailbox.

There are many variations and models of classroom walkthroughs being implemented in schools today. The Center for Comprehensive School Reform and Improvement (2007) suggests that all of the walkthrough models have three things in common: (1) brevity, (2) focus, and (3) dialogue. You may be familiar with one or more of the variations, including the Downey model (Downey et al., 2004), the Instructional Rounds model (City, Elmore, Fiarman, & Teitel, 2009), Data Walks (Learning Keys, 2010), and Learning Walks (Urban School Improvement Network, 2010).

You may also be aware of variations in school districts in which educators have adopted the concept of classroom walkthroughs and tailored it to their specific needs: Spokane School District in Washington (Sather, 2004), Palisades School District in Pennsylvania (Barnes, Miller, & Dennis, 2001), and Central Union School District in Texas (National Center for Educational Accountability, 2005).

The classroom walkthroughs model described in this book shares the characteristics of brevity, focus, and dialogue with other models, but has three features that make it unique.

1. Classroom walkthroughs using the literacy look-fors observation protocol are used to assess the *collective* instructional capacity of a group of teachers, not to evaluate and give feedback to individuals.

2. Classroom walkthroughs are a means to evaluate the effectiveness of school and district professional development initiatives and suggest further professional development needs.

3. As the principal and teachers become more comfortable with the model, classroom walkthroughs will eventually become part of every grade-level team's professional growth with teacher dialogue, both in team meetings and debriefings after walkthroughs.

Figure 2.1 summarizes the unique aspects of classroom walkthroughs as they are used in this book. In chapter 4 you will distribute copies of this chart at your faculty orientation.

Figure 2.1: What Classroom Walkthroughs Are and Are Not

Classroom walkthroughs are designed and intended to build school capacity as well as inform and evaluate professional development.
Classroom walkthroughs are not intended to provide information to be used with or for teacher supervision and evaluation.
Classroom walkthroughs do not require any advance notice to the teachers in whose classrooms the walkthroughs take place.
Classroom walkthroughs are not intended to be a professional development model for administrators, although principals will most definitely become more knowledgeable about literacy as a result of using classroom walkthroughs.
Classroom walkthroughs are not intended as a way for central office administrators to supervise either building administrators or classroom teachers.
Classroom walkthroughs are not intended as a way for central office to mandate certain procedures or artifacts in each classroom.
Classroom walkthroughs are not regularly scheduled quarterly or monthly, but occur whenever the principal is engaging in a new one-month cycle of assessing instructional capacity or the effectiveness of a professional development initiative, *or* when a collaborative grade-level team goes on a walkthrough to support their work in collaborative team meetings.
As the faculty becomes more comfortable with classroom walkthroughs, teachers will regularly go on team walkthroughs as part of their embedded professional development.
Classroom walkthroughs do not require or recommend that principals provide feedback to individual teachers. Frequency data collected by the principal will always be presented to the staff and used to plan embedded professional development and set school improvement goals.
Classroom walkthroughs encourage teachers to debrief after walkthroughs, initially with administrators or coaches during the early days of implementation, and thereafter in their teacher teams with a team leader.

Visit **go.solution-tree.com/literacy** *to download and print this figure.*

Collaborative Teacher Teams and Walkthroughs

Although you will not be taking teacher teams on walkthroughs until chapter 7, you will need to be thoroughly versed in the procedures, debriefing guidelines, and how to manage a teacher team debriefing before you conduct your teacher orientation meetings in chapter 4.

Figure 2.2 (page 50) is a set of debriefing guidelines and a confidentiality agreement for use before teacher teams begin going on classroom walkthroughs. These guidelines are amenable to change if they conflict with negotiated contracts or school district policies. Use this set of guidelines in two instances: (1) as part of the handout packet you prepare for teacher orientation in chapter 4, and (2) prior to a grade-level team's first set of classroom walkthroughs as described in chapter 7.

Figure 2.2: Debriefing Guidelines and Confidentiality Agreement

1. The debriefing meeting will last for thirty minutes. It will be chaired by the principal, coach, or team leader, depending on who led the classroom walkthrough.
2. All participants are expected to make an opening contribution to the debriefing before any other person speaks a second time. All teachers are expected to contribute before administrators.
3. Each participant will have a copy of the walkthrough learning stems. These stems are designed to scaffold reflection and discussion about observations. Participants are not required to use the learning stems during the debriefing session, but they *are* expected to contribute at least two statements relative to the literacy walkthrough experience.
4. Participants are not permitted to make any judgmental statements or offer *opinions* about what any individual teacher was doing or not doing during a classroom walkthrough. The focus must remain on the specific look-fors that were observed in the classroom.
5. After the adjournment of the debriefing meeting, all participants are expected to abide by the confidentiality statement in the professional standards agreement; they are expected not to talk outside of the debriefing meeting about anything they have seen or heard. This includes sharing any conversations from the debriefing meeting with any of the observed teachers.
6. Following the debriefing meeting, all data collection sheets and any notes participants have taken will be shredded by the principal.
I agree to honor this confidentiality agreement regarding what I have observed during classroom walkthroughs and what I have discussed during debriefing sessions with my grade-level team.
_____   _____ Name   Date

*Visit **go.solution-tree.com/literacy** to download and print this figure.*

Figure 2.3 is a set of classroom walkthrough learning stems to scaffold teacher dialogue after a teacher team walks through three classrooms together. When teachers go on their first set of classroom walkthroughs as part of the last step in chapter 7, some will feel reticent about saying anything and some will be all too ready to say the wrong things. These stems serve to keep everyone communicating in a positive way, but also have the potential to create meaningful dialogue and reflection.

The data collection form used by teacher teams for their classroom walkthroughs (shown in figure 2.4) is very simple. Teachers write in the look-fors they have chosen and answer two questions for each of the three classrooms they visit.

Following the debriefing session, participants will give their forms to the principal. The principal will shred all forms and notes. As teachers become more accustomed to the process, the principal will want to gradually release the responsibility of leading the walkthroughs and debriefing sessions to the literacy coach or team leaders. Once per month, the principal will meet with team leaders to follow-up on the team's short-term student achievement goal, future professional development needs, and an assessment about the team's efficiency and effectiveness to date.

Figure 2.3: Classroom Walkthrough Learning Stems

I am interested in how you know when you are seeing . . . I am wondering how teachers generally figure out what . . . I do not understand how some teachers . . . I am curious about why some teachers . . . and others . . . I need to know more about . . . Can you help me understand how . . . I am puzzled by the variety of ways I see . . . I have been thinking about the benefits of . . . I am interested in knowing more about . . . I am intrigued by . . . I'm eager to know . . . I am trying to make sense of . . . I am trying to comprehend . . . I am trying to solve the puzzle of . . .	I am impatient to . . . I'm hopeful that our team can . . . After this walkthrough, I'm motivated to learn more about . . . I can't wait to . . . I'm anxious to establish . . . I have recently become aware of . . . I would like to familiarize myself with . . . I would like to become more expert in . . . I would like to learn more about how to . . . I would like to gather more information about . . . I am curious about what evidence you saw of . . . . . . [a specific literacy look-for] I would like to know how you know the difference between . . . and . . . I wonder if there is a book out there about . . .

Visit **go.solution-tree.com/literacy** *to download and print this figure.*

Figure 2.4: Data Collection Form for Teacher Team Classroom Walkthroughs

Question	Classroom 1	Classroom 2	Classroom 3
Did you see any _____? Write Y (Yes) or N (No).			
What did it look like? Jot a quick note to help you remember.			

Visit **go.solution-tree.com/literacy** *to download and print this figure.*

Frequently Asked Questions From Principals About Classroom Walkthroughs

Even if you have been conducting regular walkthroughs using another model or doing them informally on your own, you may have additional questions about the look-fors and walkthroughs model used in this book. This section answers questions that arise as administrators plan to engage in classroom walkthroughs using the literacy look-fors observation protocol as their guide.

Q: I am finding it difficult when I go into classrooms to quickly scan for the literacy look-fors without slipping into my teacher evaluator mode. How can I avoid this mode of thinking?

A: The kind of judgmental stance you are slipping into is very common, and it's understandable. Principals have been trained to look for things they can write up on an evaluation form, and they have to quickly decide if this is right or wrong, positive or negative. It also leads to the mindset that that many teachers develop once you leave the classroom. They immediately think, "Am I ok?" I also see this judgmental stance in principals who want to fill out individual data sheets for each teacher and retain them in their files. You will undermine your implementation if you do not discipline yourself to stop judging. The only exception will be if you see an individual teacher doing something unsafe or harmful to students.

Q: How much time do classroom walkthroughs take every day?

A: Of course the bottom line depends on the number of classrooms you will be walking through. In the beginning you may need as much as three minutes to complete one walkthrough, but very quickly you will be able to see everything you need to see in two minutes. Here's the formula for computing the number of minutes needed daily based on the number of teachers in a school:

1. Number of teachers in school × number of visits per classroom = total number of monthly visits
   (Note that during the implementation of the seven steps, you will only engage in two one-month data collection walkthroughs. After the initial seven steps, the number of times you choose to do data collection walkthroughs will depend on whether there are professional development initiatives you want to evaluate or if grade-level teams have worked on specific achievement goals.)

2. Total number of monthly visits × total minutes per visit = total number of minutes per month

3. Total number of minutes per month ÷ 20 observation days per month = total number of minutes per day to complete walkthroughs

So, if you have 30 teachers in your school, multiply that number by 4 to calculate the total number of visits you will make in a one-month period (120 visits). In the beginning, you may take a little longer to scan the classroom looking for the indicators on your protocol. So, multiply the number of visits you will make over the month by 3 minutes for a total of 360 minutes. Now divide the total number of minutes by the number of possible visitation days in the month (20), and you will have the number of minutes per day you will need to complete your classroom walkthroughs: 18 minutes. Total daily time for both two- and three-minute walkthroughs in various sized schools is shown in figure 2.5.

Figure 2.5: Total Minutes Needed for Classroom Walkthroughs by Size of School and Length of Walkthrough

Total Number of Teachers in School	Total Minutes per Day Needed for 4 Two-Minute Walkthroughs per Month per Teacher	Total Minutes per Day Needed for 4 Three-Minute Walkthroughs per Month per Teacher
20	8 minutes	12 minutes
25	10 minutes	15 minutes
30	12 minutes	18 minutes
35	14 minutes	21 minutes
40	16 minutes	24 minutes

Q: Can I adapt the wording in certain look-fors to make them more pertinent to a certain area of the curriculum or a particular type of professional development I want to evaluate?

A: Some principals have done this with great success. The principal in the case study described in chapter 5 (page 99) at Greentree School used some variations to assess his faculty's comprehension instruction capacity. For an example of where adapting look-fors may not be acceptable, see the next Q and A.

Q: I've read through the set of teacher-managed instructional activities, and they seem rather restrictive. The teachers in my school want to differentiate in their classrooms using a combination of learning styles, reading styles, and other modalities. Is that permissible?

A: No. This *is* a nonnegotiable category based on a substantial body of research (McEwan-Adkins, 2010). Although learning styles are popular, there is no research to support their effectiveness as a way of differentiating instruction in reading. Effective literacy teachers determine which skills and strategies students do not know by examining formative and summative assessments. Then they design instruction to teach those skills and strategies, and they monitor the students' progress and response to instruction. Next, make sure their instruction is explicit, systematic, and supportive, and give the intervention time to work.

Q: I am feeling rather uncertain about my ability to interpret the results of my data collection and aggregation. It doesn't seem very scientific. Is it normal to feel like this?

A: I can appreciate what you are feeling. I would recommend teaming up with a literacy coach who spends a lot of time in classrooms and might be able to give you some perspective on what the data might mean. If you refrain from discussing individual teachers and concentrate on what the aggregated data might mean for planning professional development for teachers, this kind of discussion could be very helpful. Or, take the aggregated data to the whole faculty and share it with them. Then divide into grade-level teams and discuss what conclusions team members would draw from the data. You are looking for trends and directions to inform how to change those trends if they aren't heading in the right direction. (Note: This process is fully described and explained in chapter 5.)

Q: I am worried about how my teachers will feel if they don't happen to be implementing a specific look-for when I walk through their classrooms.

A: It sounds to me as though you are thinking about another walkthrough model you may have used in the past or even a model that you have gradually developed on your own. The big idea of literacy walkthroughs is the collection of frequency data to assess the instructional capacity of your faculty, not to bolster the morale of individual teachers with positive feedback. Hopefully your teachers will feel more motivated to intentionally incorporate the best practices described in the look-fors into their instruction so that they *will* happen to be doing the right things when you walk through. However, if you want to see the best work of a teacher, schedule an observation, hold a preobservation conference to talk about what she plans to do, and then talk after the observation to reflect on what went particularly well and how the teacher feels he or she will change anything the next time this lesson is taught. Your teachers will have four opportunities to be "caught" employing a literacy look-for during a one-month period.

Q: I feel guilty if I don't write a note of encouragement to each teacher I see on my classroom walkthroughs. Isn't it important to give teachers regular feedback?

A: The idea of writing encouraging notes sounds positive in the abstract, but over time it can become laborious and repetitive and might even discourage you from making your literacy look-fors walkthroughs in all classrooms. This model is not designed to provide teacher feedback because the principal collects data in the aggregate by tallying how often he or she sees a particular look-for during a regular monthly walkthrough. Feedback for teachers will come through another avenue—regular classroom observations that are structured to see a complete lesson from beginning to end.

Q: I find it impossible to do a quick walkthrough. I get caught up in staying to see something really good in a classroom. Is this a bad thing?

A: I used to have the same problem when I was a principal. We have classrooms that we like to hang out in. The teachers are wonderful, the lessons are divine, and we don't feel guilty when we're there. However, your job description says you have to get to every classroom at least once per week. So, get moving! This problem is like going to the store for just one thing and then wandering around the mall for hours. You are wasting time and avoiding the truly important task at hand.

Q: Do I pick certain things to look for each time I'm in the classroom, or do I have to look for everything?

A: You are in control of what you choose to look for—that is, which literacy look-fors are on your observation protocol. You and a group of literacy leaders will no doubt choose a small set of look-fors in the context of the orientation you do for the faculty in the next chapter. You will likely choose no more than four or five look-fors, particularly when you are just beginning to implement classroom walkthroughs. You will become more skilled at quickly scanning the room and leaving. If you scan the classroom and you don't see any of the look-fors listed on the protocol, the lack of data becomes a critical part of the assessment. At that point, you may decide that this teacher (or even a whole grade level) needs some coaching or embedded professional development. Sometimes as administrators we have singled out one teacher and provided coaching or professional development exclusively for them. You can't see trends unless you collect frequency data over time and over teachers. For example, one principal discovered, after collecting frequency data on the particular set of look-fors that he selected because he suspected there might be some problems, that very few of his faculty were actually teaching reading comprehension. He purchased some books and with the help of his literacy coach designed a professional growth unit that each collaborative grade-level team worked through during their planning time.

Q: What is the likelihood that my teachers could actually be doing the right things in their classrooms and I will totally miss seeing it because I am in classrooms for such a short time?

A: The solution to this issue is to develop a routine in which you vary the order in which you do your walkthroughs in different classrooms. Of course you will only go on walkthroughs during the ninety-minute literacy block, so that definitely increases the likelihood that you will see it if teachers are doing it. A second way to ensure that you get an accurate picture of what teachers are doing is to make sure you vary the time you drop by during the literacy block. If you head out to visit kindergarten classes and finish them all during the early part of the morning, make a note that the next time you want to see the kindergarten classes while they are doing Literacy Centers or when the teacher is teaching small intervention groups. Collect literacy schedules from teachers so you can vary your walkthroughs accordingly.

Q: I frequently stop in a classroom and model something for the teacher or offer some coaching advice. Is that OK?

A: There is no problem with the principal acting as a coach for teachers, particularly in a small school or district where there isn't a literacy coach or that individual's time is shared between two or three schools. However, the practice of interrupting a teacher while he or she is presenting a lesson raises questions: How can you know that coaching is indicated after two minutes? If the teaching is so bad that you have to interrupt, could it be that this teacher shouldn't be in this classroom at all? Another way to handle this is to meet with this teacher during a free period and teach and coach each other nonstop. The teacher will be more relaxed in this setting. You can specifically choose a lesson that gets at the issues this teacher has in a private coaching session. Furthermore, you can gather data from this teacher's room to be part of the overall assessment and then get on your way to the rest of your stops.

Q: My teachers want me to leave a copy of the literacy look-fors observation protocol after my walkthrough so they can see the look-fors I've checked off. They would also like me to give them written feedback. Is that okay?

A: In order to consistently conduct fast, formative, and frequent walkthroughs, the principal cannot write personal notes to every teacher. These notes soon become repetitious, and although they may give teachers a momentary glow, they do not provide the specific feedback that really improves instruction. *The literacy walkthroughs are not intended to be evaluative in nature.* The principal only collects frequency data and *never* records these data on a form containing a teacher's name. Teachers will receive reports at faculty meetings regarding the overall school findings so goals can be set and targeted professional development can be planned.

Q: Many of the walkthrough models recommend asking reflective questions of teachers. Is there a reason that it is not recommended to ask questions after literacy walkthroughs?

A: The purpose of this walkthrough model is to assess schoolwide instructional capacity, inform professional development in the school (either through the work of the literacy coach or the professional growth units), evaluate any professional development as to its impact on instruction and student learning, and grow instructional capacity through literacy growth units. The literacy look-fors observation protocol becomes the language you use in your school to talk about literacy instruction in collaborative teacher teams. Reflection takes place in those collaborative team meetings, particularly after teacher teams have gone on walkthroughs with the principal.

Q: I'm concerned about how I am going to keep my observations during the literacy walkthroughs from spilling over into my teacher evaluations. What if I see something during a walkthrough that needs to be addressed immediately? There are some things I might definitely want to keep on the table when I write my evaluation unless the teacher remediates the problem.

A: If you observe a teacher saying or doing something that needs to be addressed in a timely way (for example, disrespecting students, not following a school or district policy, and so on), you are obligated to discuss that with the teacher as soon as possible. Leave a note in the teacher's mailbox or send an email requesting a conference, and address the issue right away. This is especially important if the teacher is a new staff member. In terms of keeping the frequency data you collect during the walkthroughs and the data you collect for a teacher evaluation, you should have no problem. You are using the literacy look-fors observation protocol to collect data during two- to three-minute walkthroughs. For teacher evaluations, I am assuming you are scheduling longer periods to observe complete lessons and using your district evaluation form. The data being collected in this model are *frequency* data.

The Next Step

You are now ready to begin your preparations for orienting your faculty. This step will take careful planning as you consider your faculty, its needs, and its challenges. Whenever teachers see a long list of look-fors, they immediately think, "New evaluation system." Frequently reassure them that the literacy look-fors observation protocol is designed to assess the faculty's collective instructional capacity using frequency data.

Assess Your Instructional Leadership Capacity

Don't become mired in high-level thinking that is too broad. Follow through. Get things done. Don't let the details bore you. Follow through. Expand people's capabilities. Know thyself.

—Bossidy & Charan (2002, pp. 36, 57)

---

1. Understand the literacy look-fors.

2. Understand the classroom walkthroughs.

3. **Assess your instructional leadership capacity.**

4. Orient your faculty to the look-fors and walkthroughs.

5. Collect and analyze look-for frequency data.

6. Develop, implement, and assess embedded professional development.

7. Use team walkthroughs to build school capacity.

Your assignment for this chapter is to put yourself and your instructional leadership capacity under a microscope to determine whether you are ready to implement the look-fors and walkthroughs in your school. Specific to the issue of literacy attainment for all students is your personal instructional leadership capacity: *the ability of a principal to provide leadership directly related to the intersection and interaction of literacy standards, curriculum, instruction, and assessment that results in literacy achievement at or above grade level for all students.*

Strong instructional leadership for literacy has three distinct components: (1) a leadership component—the ability to implement, get the job done, or get results; (2) an instructional component—knowledge and skills related to literacy teaching and learning; and (3) an intensity component—assertiveness that encompasses personal attributes like self-confidence, self-differentiation, and character (McEwan, 2009a).

Following are some important questions to ask yourself as you contemplate implementing the literacy look-fors and walkthroughs in your school. Consider the list, and then we'll address each one to help you make your decision:

- ❏ Am I willing to become and remain a strong instructional leader?
- ❏ Am I willing to do the work at school?
- ❏ Am I willing to do the homework?
- ❏ Am I willing to provide time and support for collaborative teams?
- ❏ Am I willing to deal with challenging teachers?
- ❏ Am I trustworthy?

Am I Willing to Become and Remain a Strong Instructional Leader?

"A strong instructional leader provides an unequivocal direction through consistent monitoring and supervision of program implementation while simultaneously working collaboratively with teacher leaders on issues of standards, curriculum, instruction, and assessment to raise the literacy bar for all students" (McEwan, 2009a, p. 10). Only you (the principal) have the job description, the evaluative power, and the moral imperative to successfully implement the look-fors and walkthroughs. If you as the building leader do not feel passionate about literacy learning for all students, no matter what their demographics, your staff is not likely to follow where you lead. You do not have to have all of the answers before you begin.

I must forewarn you, however, that you may experience teacher pushback from two sources. First, many teachers hold an erroneous set of paradigms about literacy instruction. In order to move forward, these paradigms will have to shift. Philosopher Thomas Kuhn (1962/1996) coined the phrase *paradigm shift* to describe a fundamental change in approach or underlying assumptions that governs the behavior of an individual, group, organization, or society. Figure 3.1 shows how these paradigms will need to shift if you and your staff are going to make a lasting impact on literacy achievement for all students. You may wish to use this information to assess your staff informally through conversations at a faculty meeting, or you can use it as a tool to identify any of the beliefs and core values that may be holding your school back.

For example, the first question asks: what is the chief determinant of students' academic destiny? If you have staff members who believe that the demographics of students (income level, minority status, or English skills) determine their academic destiny, these teachers are relatively powerless to teach students whose demographics place them in categories of poverty and limited English speakers. The "right" answer is that the opportunities to learn provided in your school are the chief determinants of the literacy levels to which your students can rise. When educators cling to the obsolete paradigms of learning shown in the middle column, expect resistance. Collaborative teacher teams and literacy coaches can offer support for teachers who need knowledge and skills to help them make these paradigm shifts. However, as the principal, only you can communicate the message that teaching all students to read and write is a nonnegotiable in the school you have been hired to lead.

Figure 3.1: Paradigms That Impact Reading Achievement

The Question	Old Thinking	New Thinking
1. What is the chief determinant of students' academic destiny?	Demographics	Opportunities to learn
2. What is the most effective way to meet the needs of struggling students in kindergarten?	Waiting for students to develop	Intervention and prevention
3. How do the majority of students learn to read?	Naturally as they learn to talk	Through explicit, systematic instruction from a highly effective teacher
4. What is the most effective way to group students for reading instruction?	Whole-group instruction	Whole-group instruction and differentiated small groups
5. By what criteria should materials and instructional methods be selected?	The materials and methods with which teachers feel most comfortable	The materials and methods backed by scientifically based reading research

continued →

The Question	Old Thinking	New Thinking
6. Who is accountable for students learning to read?	Educators not accountable for students learning to read	Educators accountable for students learning to read
7. Can educators impact the chief causes of student failure?	No; most of the causes of student failure cannot be impacted by educators	Yes; educators can impact multiple variables that will result in literacy learning for all
8. In what type of environment are teachers and students most effective?	Competitive	Collaborative

Source: McEwan, 2009b.

The second possible source of pushback against your efforts to change is fear of personal attack. Some teachers strongly believe that if you (or any of their colleagues, or a reading coach, and so on) question their instructional practices, suggest more research-based and results-oriented literacy approaches, or even mandate results, you are attacking them personally. In *Instructional Rounds in Education*, City et al. (2009) clearly articulate this issue, suggesting that teachers who refuse to subscribe to the knowledge base that informs research-based reading instruction and best practices instructionally are not professional teachers:

> Professionals are not people who act according to their individual idiosyncrasies and predispositions, but people who subscribe to a common body of knowledge and a set of practices that go with that body of knowledge, and who use mastery as the basis for determining who gets to practice. (p. 160)

Teachers who resist the look-fors and walkthroughs model believe (because no one has ever challenged their beliefs) that what happens in their classrooms stays in their classrooms and is not open to observation, discussion, or question by anyone except the principal. The majority of teachers have grown accustomed to principal evaluation as the "devil they know," while anyone else observing in the classroom becomes "the devil they don't know" and poses a new threat. Many teachers like this have perfected the art of intimidating weak principals, who when confronted with an angry or aggressive teacher, simply fold and retreat to their offices to "live and let live." An assertive administrator (that's you) who suggests throwing open *their* classroom doors and inviting the faculty to walk through *their* classrooms looking for indicators of effective literacy instruction will put some of these individuals into genuine crisis mode, a moment when they are forced to become a professional teacher or choose another career option.

There will be difficult days, but keep shining a spotlight on formative and summative test data, and return—daily, if necessary—to the mantra of results. I remember a young principal in Missouri, a participant in one of my workshops, who provided the perfect comeback for his teachers who were resistant to research-based literacy instruction: "If all of your students score at the 99th percentile in reading and writing, you can be autonomous and creative, but if you have students who are failing to make grade-level standards, then you have to be open to examining your practice in a collaborative team setting and figuring out what else you can do to be more effective."

Remain strong in the face of the naysayers; resolve to become and remain a resolute and assertive instructional leader. Here are two tools that may provide some insight as to your *real* job description. Figure 3.2 sets forth the things that strong instructional leaders are doing on a daily basis. It can be used as a self-assessment process, or you can give it to faculty members to evaluate your instructional leadership. Giving faculty members an opportunity to evaluate your instructional leadership is a smart move to make as part of implementing the look-fors and walkthroughs. It communicates an openness and willingness to listen to faculty input—the same kind of reception that you hope to have from them as part of this implementation.

Figure 3.2: Instructional Leadership Behavioral Checklist

	Never	Seldom	Some-times	Usually	Always
Step 1: The strong instructional leader establishes, implements, and achieves academic standards.					
Indicator 1.1: Incorporates the designated state and district standards into the development and implementation of the local school's instructional programs	1	2	3	4	5
Indicator 1.2: Ensures that schoolwide and individual classroom instructional activities are consistent with state, district, and school standards and are aligned with one another	1	2	3	4	5

continued →

	Never	Seldom	Some-times	Usually	Always
Indicator 1.3: Uses multiple sources of data, both qualitative and quantitative, to evaluate progress and plan for continuous improvement	1	2	3	4	5
Indicator 1.4: Provides instructional leadership that results in meaningful and measurable achievement gains	1	2	3	4	5
Step 2: The strong instructional leader is an instructional resource for staff.					
Indicator 2.1: Works with teachers to improve the instructional program in their classrooms consistent with student needs	1	2	3	4	5
Indicator 2.2: Facilitates instructional program development based on trustworthy research and proven instructional practices	1	2	3	4	5
Indicator 2.3: Uses appropriate formative assessment procedures and informal data collection methods for evaluating the effectiveness of instructional programs in achieving state, district, and local standards	1	2	3	4	5
Step 3: The strong instructional leader creates a school climate and culture conducive to learning.					
Indicator 3.1: Establishes high expectations for student achievement that are directly communicated to students, teachers, and parents	1	2	3	4	5
Indicator 3.2: Establishes clear standards, communicates high expectations for the use of time allocated to various content areas, and monitors the effective use of classroom time	1	2	3	4	5
Indicator 3.3: With teachers and students (as appropriate), establishes, implements, and evaluates the procedures and codes for handling and correcting behavior problems	1	2	3	4	5

	Never	Seldom	Some-times	Usually	Always
Step 4: The strong instructional leader communicates the vision and mission of the school.					
Indicator 4.1: Provides for systematic two-way communication with staff regarding achievement standards and the improvement goals of the school	1	2	3	4	5
Indicator 4.2: Establishes, supports, and implements activities that communicate the value and meaning of learning to students	1	2	3	4	5
Indicator 4.3: Develops and uses communication channels with parents to set forth school objectives	1	2	3	4	5
Step 5: The strong instructional leader sets high expectations for staff and self.					
Indicator 5.1: Assists teachers yearly in setting and reaching personal and professional goals related to the improvement of instruction, student achievement, and professional development	1	2	3	4	5
Indicator 5.2: Makes regular classroom observations in all classrooms, both informal (drop-in visits of varying length with no written or verbal feedback to teacher) and formal (visits during which observation data are recorded and communicated to teacher)	1	2	3	4	5
Indicator 5.3: Engages in planning with teacher prior to classroom observations	1	2	3	4	5
Indicator 5.4: Engages in post-observation conferences that focus on the improvement of instruction	1	2	3	4	5
Indicator 5.5: Provides thorough, defensible, and insightful evaluations, making recommendations for personal and professional growth goals according to individual needs	1	2	3	4	5

continued →

	Never	Seldom	Some-times	Usually	Always
Indicator 5.6: Engages in direct teaching in the classroom	1	2	3	4	5
Indicator 5.7: Holds high expectations for personal instructional leadership behavior, regularly solicits feedback (both formal and informal) from staff members regarding instructional leadership abilities, and uses such feedback to set yearly performance goals	1	2	3	4	5
Step 6: The strong instructional leader develops teacher leaders.					
Indicator 6.1: Schedules, plans, or facilitates regular meetings of all types (planning, problem solving, decision making, or inservice training) with and among teachers to address instructional issues	1	2	3	4	5
Indicator 6.2: Provides opportunities for and training in collaboration, shared decision making, coaching, mentoring, curriculum development, and presentations	1	2	3	4	5
Indicator 6.3: Provides motivation and resources for faculty members to engage in professional growth activities	1	2	3	4	5
Step 7: The strong instructional leader establishes and maintains positive relationships with students, parents, and teachers.					
Indicator 7.1: Serves as an advocate for students, and communicates with them regarding their school life	1	2	3	4	5
Indicator 7.2: Encourages open communication among staff members, and maintains respect for differences of opinion	1	2	3	4	5
Indicator 7.3: Demonstrates concern and openness in the consideration of teacher, parent, and student problems, and participates in the resolution of such problems when appropriate	1	2	3	4	5

	Never	Seldom	Some-times	Usually	Always
Indicator 7.4: Models appropriate human relations skills	1	2	3	4	5
Indicator 7.5: Develops and maintains high morale	1	2	3	4	5
Indicator 7.6: Systematically collects and responds to staff, parent, and student concerns	1	2	3	4	5
Indicator 7.7: Acknowledges appropriately the meaningful accomplishments of others	1	2	3	4	5

Source: McEwan, 2002a. Visit **go.solution-tree.com/literacy** *to download and print this figure.*

Figure 3.3 is designed for self-evaluation. Use this tool and the instructional leadership checklist to remind you of what's important. Yes, the buses, budgets, and boilers are necessary—but without student learning, they are meaningless.

Figure 3.3: The Assertive Administrator Self-Assessment

	Never	Seldom	Some-times	Usually	Always
Indicator 1: I protect and honor my own rights as an individual as well as the rights of teachers.	1	2	3	4	5
Indicator 2: I recognize the importance of boundaries and am able to stay connected to others while at the same time maintaining a sense of self and individuality.	1	2	3	4	5
Indicator 3: I have positive feelings regarding myself and am thus able to create positive feelings in teachers.	1	2	3	4	5
Indicator 4: I am willing to take risks, but recognize that mistakes and failures are part of the learning process.	1	2	3	4	5

continued →

	Never	Seldom	Some-times	Usually	Always
Indicator 5: I am able to acknowledge and learn from my successes as well as my failures.	1	2	3	4	5
Indicator 6: I am able to give and receive both compliments and constructive criticism from teachers.	1	2	3	4	5
Indicator 7: I make realistic promises and commitments to teachers and am able to keep them.	1	2	3	4	5
Indicator 8: I genuinely respect the ideas and feelings of teachers.	1	2	3	4	5
Indicator 9: I am willing to compromise and negotiate with teachers in good faith.	1	2	3	4	5
Indicator 10: I am capable of saying no to teachers and sticking to a position, but I do not need to have my own way at all costs.	1	2	3	4	5
Indicator 11: I can handle anger, hostility, put-downs, and lies from teachers without undue distress, recognizing that I am defined from within.	1	2	3	4	5
Indicator 12: I can handle anger, hostility, put-downs, and lies from teachers without responding in kind.	1	2	3	4	5
Indicator 13: I am aware of my personal emotions (such as anger or anxiety), can name them, and can manage them in both myself and teachers.	1	2	3	4	5
Indicator 14: I am prepared for and can cope with the pain that is a normal part of leading a school.	1	2	3	4	5

Source: McEwan, 2005. Visit **go.solution-tree.com/literacy** *to download and print this figure.*

Am I Willing to Do the Work at School?

Classroom walkthroughs present you with a unique opportunity to raise literacy achievement in your school. This is done by building instructional capacity through an ongoing cycle of assessment, embedded professional development, goal setting, and further assessment to see how teachers are implementing what they have learned during their collaborative team meetings. However, you cannot fully implement literacy look-fors and walkthroughs without being a hands-on instructional leader. This model requires that you visit classrooms every day (not all classrooms, but some), look for indicators that make for outstanding literacy achievement, collect frequency data on the look-fors, lead grade-level teams on walkthroughs, and then debrief with them in team meetings. Monitor collaborative teams by dropping in on meetings, encourage and affirm their work, and offer trouble-shooting and problem-solving resources. Collaborative teams will grow the instructional capacity of your school. The look-fors and walkthroughs are designed to keep you and your faculty focused on what's important. However, you must breathe energy, motivation, and expectation into the model for it to bear the fruits of high literacy attainment for all students.

Am I Willing to Do the Homework?

Implementing the literacy look-fors and walkthroughs requires more than wandering around looking for signs of literacy instruction: it also involves homework. You must become knowledgeable about the literacy look-fors through a careful study of chapter 1. Walk through classrooms looking for the indicators until you feel comfortable that you can identify examples and non-examples of the look-fors and can speak descriptively about the look-fors in faculty meetings and visits to grade-level team meetings. I suggest working through the look-fors with your literacy coach or a group of administrators to help you more completely process the concepts and information.

Am I Willing to Provide Time and Support for Collaborative Teams?

Collaboration is the heart of the classroom walkthrough model and is essential to building instructional capacity. To implement look-fors and walkthroughs, each grade-level team needs sufficient time in which to collaboratively work through embedded professional development activities, take monthly classroom walkthroughs with administrators and literacy coaches, plan and teach model lessons, and set monthly student learning goals. If collaborative team time is not currently part of your school schedule, do some juggling to make it happen. If grade-level teams have not been using their team time in positive and productive ways, put them on notice that literacy achievement requires the meeting of great minds and that those great minds can no longer work in isolation.

Collaboration is powerful when the goal is challenging and calls for a variety of talents, essential when different points of view and thinking styles are needed to accomplish a task, and empowering when all group members can do their best work without fear of failure. However, the trump card of collaboration is that it is the *only* way a diverse faculty with diverse students can hope to achieve the alignment of content standards, curriculum, instruction, and assessment needed to raise the literacy achievement bar for all students.

Am I Willing to Deal With Challenging Teachers?

It is the responsibility of administrators to deal with teachers who are unwilling or even unable to grow professionally. A collaborative team can only go so far to support, motivate, and empower dysfunctional teammates. However, in many cases, teachers need to step up and hold their colleagues accountable. Disgruntled teachers who are keeping their teams from professional growth and are undermining the academic mission of the school need a dose of tough love and an assertive intervention from fellow team members. Allow me (as a former principal) to give teacher teams permission to put "telling the truth in love" on the next team agenda. Principals can and should have straightforward conversations with dysfunctional and marginal teachers. However, in many instances, the truth is far more powerful when delivered in the context of a team meeting with peers.

Michael Fullan challenges principals:

> The biggest dilemma facing all leaders with moral purpose is what to do if you don't trust the competence and motivation of the people you are expected to lead. . . . Leaders need to take action to counsel out or otherwise rid the schools of teachers who persistently neglect their own learning. (2003, p. 66)

Courageous principals need to tackle the toughest challenges. Teacher leaders need to step up and help their principals with this task.

Am I Trustworthy?

Relational trust is essential to a successful implementation of the look-fors and walkthroughs model. The research of Anthony Bryk and Barbara

Schneider (2002) confirms the impossibility of improving schools without the presence of relational trust. As a result of extensive case studies and survey analyses in twelve Chicago public schools undergoing reform, they concluded that trust was essential for turning schools around. In addition to marked improvements in academic productivity, Bryk and Schneider also cite the following benefits of trust:

> Collective decision making with broad teacher buy-in occurs more readily in schools with strong relational trust.
>
> When relational trust is strong, change and improvement are likely to be firmly supported by school participants and to be diffused broadly across the school.
>
> Relational trust generates a moral imperative to take on the hard work of school improvement—doing more and working longer hours without regard for the job description or the contract. (2002, pp. 122–123)

How can you, one principal, build trust in a school community if it is filled with difficult people, negative attitudes, and distrust? Begin with yourself. You are the role model for trustworthiness, and your faculty will take its lead from you. The rules that govern how people behave, treat one another, and solve difficult problems in a school are often unwritten, creating multiple possibilities for misunderstanding, conflict, and distrust. In a toxic school culture, the rules protect the status quo and perpetuate negative attitudes and behaviors. If you have not been a character builder, begin today to ask for forgiveness and rebuild your reputation with your faculty. It's never too late.

The Next Step

Now that you have assessed your personal leadership capacity and taken time (if needed) to address some important issues, you are ready to orient your faculty to the look-fors and walkthroughs.

Chapter **4**

Orient Your Faculty to the Look-Fors and Walkthroughs

If the school is the unit of improvement, then individual teachers have to work across classrooms to generate improvement. One classroom at a time won't work.

—City et al. (2009, p. 162)

1. Understand the literacy look-fors.

2. Understand the classroom walkthroughs.

3. Assess your instructional leadership capacity.

4. **Orient your faculty to the look-fors and walkthroughs.**

5. Collect and analyze look-for frequency data.

6. Develop, implement, and assess embedded professional development.

7. Use team walkthroughs to build school capacity.

In this chapter you will find suggestions for orienting your teachers to the look-fors and walkthroughs. Take your time with the orientation process. Make sure your faculty thoroughly understands the look-fors and walkthroughs and begins to see the potential they have for connecting faculty professional growth to student learning.

The key to any successful improvement implementation depends on a combination of embedded professional development activities and total principal commitment. Even if you receive help from central office or a jump-start from out-of-district providers, your implementation is not likely to achieve its intended results unless you are leading the team, articulating your expectations, and taking risks alongside your teachers. Therefore, *you* are in charge of providing the orientation to the literacy look-fors and walkthroughs to your faculty.

Ideally, the introduction will take place in three orientation sessions, each one sixty to ninety minutes long. However, no matter how carefully you plan, roadblocks can pop up to slow your progress. Knowing what the roadblocks might be in advance of implementation won't solve all of your problems, but advance warning can help you thoroughly prepare for your orientation sessions to minimize problems.

Roadblocks to Implementation

Here are the most common roadblocks to a successful implementation of the literacy look-fors and walkthroughs:

- ❏ Lack of principal preparation
- ❏ Lack of collaborative teacher team meeting time
- ❏ The "Julie Andrews Syndrome"
- ❏ Collective bargaining issues
- ❏ Inadequate professional development for staff
- ❏ Lack of teacher buy-in
- ❏ Lack of schoolwide academic focus and purpose
- ❏ Confusion about the use of the data
- ❏ Lack of relational trust

Consider each of these roadblocks as they apply to the culture and climate of your school, prioritizing those that must be strategically dismantled or circumvented to keep your implementation moving forward.

Lack of Principal Preparation

If you have read and cognitively processed the introduction and chapters 1–3, your personal preparation is well underway. If, however, you have skimmed through the first half of the book in anticipation of orienting your staff tomorrow, your lack of knowledge and skills may derail your implementation before it starts. Many initiatives, from local to federal nationwide reforms, have failed to bring about increases in student achievement because principals were not adequately prepared. If you want your teachers to change, you must be willing to learn, grow, and change in tandem with them on a reasonable timetable.

Lack of Collaborative Teacher Team Meeting Time

Thus far we have not fully explored the role of collaborative teacher teams in the literacy walkthroughs implementation. But they play a major role, and to do that they need dedicated meeting time for collaboration. If you do not have time specifically allocated to team meetings, you will not be able to maximize the power of the look-fors and walkthroughs. Make time for teachers to engage in professional growth.

The "Julie Andrews Syndrome"

Many districts and schools have gone to great lengths to provide dedicated time for collaborative grade-level team meetings assuming that once teacher teams have the time, they will know how to use it productively to focus on issues of teaching and learning. However, some teacher teams have what I call the "Julie Andrews Syndrome": they use their meeting time to talk about their favorite things, issues that may have little to do with growing their own instructional and leadership capacities, to say nothing of increasing their students' academic capacities. Unfocused teams need embedded professional development, principal monitoring, and accountability for how they spend their time.

Collective Bargaining Issues

If your district is located in a state in which collective bargaining is mandated, you are no doubt familiar with the parameters of your teachers' contract. Teacher evaluation is always at the top of the union's list during bargaining. The beauty of classroom walkthroughs is that they are conducted solely for the purpose of assessing buildingwide instructional capacity. The information you collect during walkthroughs never becomes part of a teacher's personnel file because the data collection checksheets do not contain names of teachers or grade levels. This is a pledge you must make to your faculty during the orientation. If you break your promise, your look-fors and walkthroughs implementation will self-destruct. The figure called What Classroom Walkthroughs Are and Are Not (figure 2.1, page 49) contains a set of statements that are available for download at **go.solution-tree.com/literacy**. You may want to use this during your orientation to clarify exactly what you do and do not intend to do.

Inadequate Professional Development for Staff

Many classroom walkthrough models do not provide training for teachers. Staff are simply given a protocol and expected to translate what it says into teacher-friendly language they can apply to their instruction. The rationale in some approaches seems to be that giving teachers a list of look-fors will force them into compliance. However, what often results is that teachers pay cynical lip service to a mandate that has no connection to professional growth or student learning. When your teachers leave your orientation meeting, they should have no doubts about your intentions or the goal of the look-fors and walkthroughs.

Lack of Teacher Buy-In

Nothing can sabotage an implementation more quickly than lack of teacher buy-in. This lack of support is often related to two previous road-blocks: inadequate professional development for teachers and teachers' beliefs about literacy instruction. Some reformers require that 80 percent or more of teachers agree to support an initiative or school improvement goal before they will work with a school. There is a dynamic at work in many schools, particularly dysfunctional ones, in which a critical mass of teachers feel a sense of entitlement in terms of what should be taught and how it should be done. As principal, be prepared for such eventualities, and reread the section in chapter 2 about how to be an assertive principal.

Lack of Schoolwide Academic Focus and Purpose

One of my favorite aphorisms comes from the late John Wooden, legendary basketball coach at UCLA. He frequently reminded his teams at practice, "Do not mistake activity for achievement" (Wooden, 1997, p. 201). When activity overrides academic achievement, there is usually a leadership vacuum. When the leadership capacity is depleted, instructional capacity similarly declines. When instructional capacity is debilitated, academic capacity virtually disappears. Without academic capacity, students are unable to acquire the abilities to read and write at and above grade level. Mistaking activity for achievement is symptomatic of districts and schools that are teacher-centered rather than student- and learning-centered. This issue may have to be addressed head-on before you begin your implementation or approached more systemically as you begin to use the look-fors and walkthroughs.

Confusion About the Use of Data

Collecting frequency data to assess instructional capacity is often a new concept to teachers. Based on their prior experiences, they have a difficult time believing that the literacy look-fors observation protocol hasn't been devised to inspect and evaluate their instruction, or to catch them not doing what they are supposed to be doing. They don't believe that principals can collect data about instruction that won't be reflected in their summative evaluations. Spend as much time as needed to address this confusion and to convince them of your intentions.

You may also need to clarify the difference between serious problems in a classroom that must be addressed immediately and everything else you see during classroom walkthroughs. Here is an example that I use with teachers when I am addressing this question: "If I walk through your classroom during the literacy block and notice that the extension cord you have connected from your computer to the outlet is a safety hazard for students walking to the bookshelf, I will quietly correct that problem and make a note to talk to you about it later. If I return the following day to find the extension cord once again draped across the aisle where students are walking, I will assume insubordination and write a letter of reprimand."

Another example I use with teachers is this: "If, when I'm in your classroom looking for indicators of excellent literacy instruction, I see you touch a child inappropriately or use demeaning language that is not acceptable in the classroom, I will leave a note in your mailbox requesting that you see me before you leave for the day."

Reasonable professionals understand that there are certain behaviors that cannot be ignored, even overnight. Teachers who are unable or unwilling to react appropriately to the principal's firm directive to eliminate this kind of behavior have "asked for" a letter of reprimand in their mailbox with a copy placed in the personnel file. Although you have promised the faculty that nothing you see during a literacy walkthrough will be included in their evaluations, that does not include any actions or words that impact the safety and well-being of students.

Lack of Relational Trust

As noted earlier in chapter 3, the research of Bryk and Schneider (2002) confirms the impossibility of improving schools without the presence of relational trust. They concluded that trust was a core resource, essential for turning schools around. Those of us who have facilitated improvement or been part of a total turnaround in a low-performing school know that eventually things will get better, but that in the beginning, "leaders must settle for far less than universal affection. They must accept conflict. They must be able and willing to be unloved" (Burns, 1978, p. 34).

Teacher Orientation for Look-Fors and Walkthroughs

The teacher orientation you provide for the look-fors and walkthroughs will take place in three meetings. Here is a brief overview of each one. More detail will be provided after the handouts are explained.

1. The first meeting will be informational in nature, explaining the nuts and bolts of look-fors and walkthroughs, providing definitions for terms that may be new to teachers, and answering the questions they have. During this meeting, staff members will also complete an assessment of the school's literacy program (figure 4.2, page 82). The information gathered from this survey will reveal your staff's perceptions regarding literacy instruction in your school and give you data to inform further discussions. Be sure to include all of your school's specialists in this orientation meeting. Even if these individuals are shared with other schools, their specialized knowledge will be invaluable to you and your faculty as you implement the look-fors and walkthroughs.

2. During the second orientation meeting, you will accomplish two tasks: (1) report to the faculty on the results and implications of the literacy assessment they completed during the first meeting, and (2) select a small number of look-fors using the Affinity Process that will become part of your first set of classroom walkthroughs in chapter 5.

3. During the third orientation meeting, engage in one of two process activities to address or identify issues you believe have the potential to derail your implementation. If you choose to use both of these process activities, a fourth meeting will be required.

Prepare the Handouts for Orienting Your Faculty

You have two choices when it comes to preparing handouts for faculty orientation: (1) give teachers all of the handouts they will need for all three meetings at the first session, or (2) pass out handouts as needed for each meeting. There are pros and cons to full disclosure—not the least of which is those teachers who lose things—but I favor it nonetheless. Teachers need and deserve to have the big picture from the beginning.

Figure 4.1 contains a complete list of the handouts needed for the three orientation meetings. Many of the listed figures appeared in earlier chapters. The handouts are listed in roughly the order they will be needed. However, you have the option to use the handouts in other ways that better meet your needs and those of your teachers. Photocopy the handouts on three–hole paper for insertion into a notebook or folder (visit **go.solution–tree.com /literacy** to download and print forms).

Figure 4.1: Teacher Handouts

Title of Handout	Figure # Page #	Purpose
Seven Steps to Effective Implementation	Figure I.2, p. 6	This handout is an organizer that gives both you and your teachers a way to remember the various implementation steps.
Definitions of Key Concepts	Figure I.1, p. 3	This handout contains definitions of all of the specialized terms used in the book. You may wish to tell teachers that you will be going over these as they come up in the discussion, but they are free, of course, to read the entire handout independently.
Suggested Implementation Timeline	Figure I.3, p. 9	This handout describes a suggested timeline. If you are planning to utilize another timeline, you may wish to omit this figure from the Teacher Orientation Packet.
The Five Categories of Literacy Look-Fors	Figure 1.1, p. 14	This handout provides a quick look at the definitions for each of the look-fors categories.
Complete Literacy Look-Fors Observation Protocol	Figure 1.1.1	Visit **go.solution-tree.com /literacy** to download and print this figure. It is not available in the text of the book.
Complete Literacy Look-Fors Exemplars and Nonexemplars	Figure 1.1.2	Visit **go.solution-tree.com /literacy** to download and print this figure. It is not available in the text of the book.
What Classroom Walkthroughs Are and Are Not	Figure 2.1, p. 49	Your teachers will need this information immediately. After the orientation (described in this chapter) you will begin your one-month set of walkthroughs to collect frequency data (described in chapter 5).

continued →

Title of Handout	Figure # Page #	Purpose
Debriefing Guidelines and Confidentiality Agreement	Figure 2.2, p. 50	This information will not be needed until you reach the last step of implementation in chapter 7, but having it in the handout packet will give teachers an opportunity to process and think about it.
Classroom Walkthrough Learning Stems	Figure 2.3, p. 51	This handout will not be used until the final step of implementation (described in chapter 7).
Data Collection Form for Teacher Team Classroom Walkthroughs	Figure 2.4, p. 51	This data collection form will not be used until the final step of implementation.
School Literacy Program Assessment	Figure 4.2, p. 82	Do not include this figure in the handout packet. Once teachers fill it out during the first orientation meeting, you will collect the forms and collate the scores.
Affinity Process Diagram	Figure 4.3, p. 85	This form will be used by the whole staff to identify the look-fors to be used in the first set of classroom walkthroughs.
Sample Grade-Level Team Professional Standards Code	Figure 4.5, p. 87	This figure is used in the Professional Standards Code process. The facilitator of the process will cut the figure into strips to be placed into envelopes as part of the process.
Directions for the Professional Standards Process	Figure 4.6, p. 89	These directions will guide the development of the Professional Standards Code during the third orientation meeting.
Force Field Analysis Worksheet	Figure 4.7, p. 90	Participants will complete this worksheet in small groups, and their information will be collated into one list representing the entire group's ideas.

*Visit **go.solution-tree.com/literacy** to download and print this figure.*

Orientation Meeting #1: Understand the Look-Fors and Walkthroughs

Agenda

1. Based on your experiences as you worked your way through chapters 1–3, select and introduce the key concepts found in the Definitions of Key Concepts handout (figure I.1, page 3) that you feel your teachers need to know immediately. There is no need to go over every definition since many of them will not be relevant at the outset. However, you and they will definitely need the definitions throughout the orientation meetings and the implementation.

2. Explain the literacy look-fors and walkthroughs process using Seven Steps to Effective Implementation (figure I.2, page 6). Describe the first three steps that you have taken as principal to prepare for the implementation through reading, study, and self-assessments. Share some new insights and ideas you have come upon that you think will activate and motivate your staff.

3. Offer, make, and discuss your pledge regarding the statements in the handout What Classroom Walkthroughs Are and Are Not (figure 2.1, page 49). After making your pledge, address any questions teachers have.

4. Introduce the figure called The Five Categories of Literacy Look-Fors (figure 1.1, page 14). Assure teachers that at no time will you be looking for all of the indicators at once. Nor, at any time, would you expect to see all sixty items at once. Explain to teachers that during the next orientation meeting, you will be engaging the staff in a process to determine which look-fors they believe may be the strongest in their classrooms, and which ones they feel need to be encouraged, supported, and even developed through embedded professional development.

5. Lay out the ground rules for classroom walkthroughs, their purpose, and the role that teachers will play using What Classroom Walkthroughs Are and Are Not (figure 2.1, page 49), Debriefing Guidelines and Confidentiality Agreement (figure 2.2, page 50), Classroom Walkthroughs Learning Stems (figure 2.3, page 51), and Data Collection Form for Teacher Team Classroom Walkthroughs (figure 2.4, page 51). Also explain that eventually (months down the

road, but nevertheless in the plan) teachers will open their classrooms to walkthroughs by their colleagues.

6. Take time to answer questions. Continue to reassure staff that you and they are taking this one step at a time, and that they will always be kept informed of the next step in plenty of time to get ready for it.

7. You will probably not answer every question or allay every fear. At the point when questions have become repetitious, it's time to conclude that part of the meeting and distribute the literacy program evaluation shown in figure 4.2. Do not include this handout in the packet you distribute to teachers at the beginning of the meeting. You will collect a completed form from every teacher and give them to clerical staff, who will compute the average score for each individual item and an average overall score.

Figure 4.2: School Literacy Program Assessment

Directions: *Circle the number that best describes the status of the following indicators in your school.*

	Not Present	Struggling	Improving	Strong	Very Strong
Indicator 1 Strong instructional leadership and shared decision making by administrators and teacher leaders	1	2	3	4	5
Indicator 2 High expectations and accountability for students, teachers, and parents—a sense of academic press that is shared and supported by the entire school community, including the school board	1	2	3	4	5
Indicator 3 A relentless commitment to results driven by meaningful and measurable short- and long-term goals	1	2	3	4	5

	Not Present	Struggling	Improving	Strong	Very Strong
Indicator 4 Research-based curricula for the essential curricular components of literacy	1	2	3	4	5
Indicator 5 A coordinated and articulated instructional delivery system that addresses the needs of struggling as well as accelerated students	1	2	3	4	5
Indicator 6 A comprehensive progress-monitoring and assessment system using technically sound instruments	1	2	3	4	5
Indicator 7 A dedication to allocating, using, and protecting time for literacy instruction	1	2	3	4	5
Indicator 8 A seamless integration and coordination of special services with classroom instruction to include special education, Title I, English learners, speech, and language services	1	2	3	4	5
Indicator 9 Teacher collaboration in grade-level teams at least twice weekly during regularly allocated teacher team time	1	2	3	4	5

continued →

	Not Present	Struggling	Improving	Strong	Very Strong
Indicator 10 Ongoing and meaningful embedded professional growth opportunities as well as targeted growth opportunities for individuals or grade levels as needed	1	2	3	4	5
Indicator 11 Support of parents and community	1	2	3	4	5
Indicator 12 Adequate and sustained resources	1	2	3	4	5

*Source: Adapted from McEwan, 2002b. Visit **go.solution-tree.com/literacy** to download and print this figure.*

Orientation Meeting #2: Choose A Set of Literacy Look-Fors for the Walkthroughs

Agenda

1. Report to the faculty on the results of the Literacy Program Evaluation. If you are puzzled about any of the results, discuss them with your literacy team to determine what steps, if any, you might recommend when discussing the results. If you find problems, consider using them as the basis for the Force Field Analysis process (figure 4.7, page 90) at the final orientation meeting.

2. Use the Affinity Process to select individual look-fors for the principal's first set of walkthroughs.

Select the Pilot Look-Fors Using the Affinity Process

The Affinity Process is a converging process (sixty minutes) in which small groups of faculty members take a large number of items (in this case, the forty-eight literacy look-fors in categories 1–4) and group them under agreed-upon headers using sticky notes. This process enables a large group of people (from twenty-five to fifty) to quickly determine their instructional concerns. Explain to staff that you are not including the twelve look-fors from the Classroom Artifacts category because they are less amenable to the kind of deeper study and conversation you hope staff will engage in during their embedded professional development project (chapter 6).

You will need chart paper, colored markers, and sticky notes.

1. Create an organizer for the wall using a piece of chart paper with the following headings: Look-Fors That Are Missing, Look-Fors That Need Supervision, Look-Fors That Are High Yield, and Look-Fors We Have Under Control, similar to the sample found in figure 4.3.

2. Divide into small groups of four to six individuals. If you have a small faculty with two or fewer teachers at a grade level, divide into grade-level teams.

3. Ask each group to choose a facilitator.

4. Give each individual a copy of the Complete Literacy Look-Fors Exemplars and Nonexemplars (figure 1.1.2). Remember that this particular figure is only available for download and does not appear in the text of the book.

Figure 4.3: Affinity Process Diagram

	Look-Fors We Have Under Control	
Look-Fors That Need Supervision		**Look-Fors That Are High Yield**
	Look-Fors That Are Missing	

Source: Adapted from McEwan (1997). Visit **go.solution-tree.com/literacy** *to download and print this figure.*

Give each staff member a copy of the process directions shown in figure 4.4. This step will save you having to repeat the directions orally.

Figure 4.4: Directions for the Affinity Process

1.	Review each literacy look-for in the first four categories of the Complete Literacy Look-Fors Exemplars and Nonexemplars (figure 1.1.2).
2.	Categorize each look-for into one of the four categories on the Affinity Process diagram found in figure 4.3 (page 85). Put an *M* in front of each look-for that you know is missing in your classroom and believe may be missing in other classrooms in the school based on conversations and observations. Put an *S* in front of each look-for that you think could benefit from more supervision, coaching, or professional development in your classroom (or in other classrooms in the school) based on your conversations and observations. Write *MA* in front of each look-for that you believe you and most other teachers in the building are implementing. Put a *Y* in front of any look-for that you think, if faithfully implemented buildingwide, would yield an immediate boost in student achievement.
3.	Once your group has coded all of the look-fors, choose the look-for in each category that received the most votes.
4.	Once each group or team has placed a sticky note in each category, take a moment for teachers to inspect the final product on the wall.
5.	See if there are any conclusions you can draw or inferences you can make about which four look-fors the principal should select for the pilot walkthroughs.

Orientation Meeting #3: Use a Group Process to Build Capacity

This section contains two group processes to use as needed: the Professional Standards Code process and the Force Field Analysis process. Note that each process requires a full meeting of at least sixty to ninety minutes to complete.

The first process will help your faculty reach consensus on professional behavioral expectations. If the climate and culture have been declining or you are relatively new to a school in which the culture is a bit toxic, you may wish to use the process to refresh people's minds about how professional teachers are expected to treat one another. The second process will help you and your educators address a serious problem that may exist by laying out on the table the variables that are contributing to the problem and those that might facilitate solving the problem.

Professional Standards Code

One way to build trust anew in a group of distrustful individuals is by giving staff members the responsibility to develop a professional standards document that formalizes a set of expectations governing teachers' professional conduct. This process (sixty to ninety minutes) and the resulting set of standards will reset the rules that govern interpersonal relationships in your school and establish a new set of expectations for collaborative grade-level teams. The process will also create, nurture, and monitor positive and professional staff behaviors and attitudes.

At the principal's discretion, participants will work in either groups of five to eight individuals from various grade levels or in grade-level teams. Make one copy of the Sample Grade-Level Team Professional Standards Code (figure 4.5) for each group. Cut apart the phrases in the right-hand column, and place all of them into an envelope. At the end of this copying and cutting process, you should have as many envelopes as you have groups of five to eight, each one containing separate strips of all of the phrases from the sample professional standards document.

Figure 4.5: Sample Grade-Level Team Professional Standards Code

Our faculty will build and maintain respectful, collaborative, and professional relationships by exhibiting the following attitudes and behaviors.	
Interpersonal Relations	Trusting and respecting each other and accommodating diverse personalities and thinking styles
	Recognizing that each staff member brings an educational background, professional experience, and compilation of life skills that are unique and valuable to our team
	Modeling forgiveness by letting go of past hurts and working actively to build and maintain healthy relationships
	Practicing positive decision making through nondivisive strategies, compromise, and respect for different points of view
Professional Growth	Supporting each other's professional growth through active participation in literacy walkthroughs and professional growth units
	Moving from thinking as individuals with complete curricular and instructional autonomy to grade-level teams with collective instructional capacity and accountability
	Improving literacy instruction throughout the school by sharing research-based instructional activities and materials
	Being accountable as both individuals and as a team for the literacy learning of our students
	Moving from regarding the practice of teaching as a private and personal part of one's identity to working collaboratively to improve our practice of teaching
	Speaking with candor about practices that are not research based and not in the best interests of students

continued →

Communication	Respecting total confidentiality regarding observations made during literacy walkthroughs and conversations held during debriefing sessions
	Using face-to-face communication and conflict-resolution strategies—such as giving "I" messages—when concerns arise
	Using conflict-mediation strategies—including the option of using facilitators—to clear up misunderstandings and resolve conflicts
	Keeping open lines of communication between individuals and groups of staff members
	Being professional in nonverbal, verbal, and written communications
Decision Making	Seeking input from all team members regarding decisions that affect those members
	Using nondivisive strategies to enhance positive decision making (for example, decision by consensus, surveys, trouble-shooting committees, and so on)
	Making every effort to reach acceptable compromises and avoiding decisions that divide the staff by giving ample time for discussion so that consensus can be reached
Team Meeting Norms	Respecting the opportunities of team members to learn in team meetings by arriving and adjourning on time, completing assigned readings and other tasks, refraining from sidebar conversations, and resisting the use of cell phones to talk, text or browse the Internet
	Respecting the responsibilities of each member to participate by expecting everyone to contribute before any single person makes another contribution
	Agreeing that our highest priority is student learning, a goal that takes precedence over personal preferences and individual styles

Source: Adapted from McEwan, 2005. Visit **go.solution-tree.com/literacy** *to download and print this figure.*

Direct each team or group to select a facilitator (for example, the person with most years of teaching experience) and a recorder (for example, the person with the smallest pet).

Then give each group a piece of chart paper and enough copies of figure 4.6 for all members. Take a moment for teachers to review the steps and check as to their understanding. Allocate forty minutes for this process. It may conclude before all of the time is used, or it may extend somewhat longer. The need for this process depends on the makeup of the teams, the culture of your school, and the trust levels between and among teachers and administrators.

Force Field Analysis

If you sense that there are forces in your school working against your goal of literacy for all or you have uncovered a more serious problem in the Literacy Program Evaluation, consider using a process called the Force Field Analysis. It

Figure 4.6: Directions for the Professional Standards Process

1.	Facilitator: Take the enclosed strips of paper from the envelope. Each strip has a different behavioral expectation written on it.
2.	Facilitator: Ask the group, "Do we want this expectation to be part of our professional standards document?"
3.	Recorder: If your group accepts the statement as written, tape it on the chart paper provided.
4.	Facilitator: If your group wants to revise or edit the statement, do so *before* you tape it on the chart paper.
5.	Facilitator: If your group does not want this statement to be a part of your Professional Standards Code, lay it aside in a separate pile.
6.	Group members: Review the list you have created. Are there any other revisions to make or any behavioral expectations that you want to add?
7.	Recorder: Make a list of all the statements, including the revised ones.
8.	Group members: As you consider these statements, which ones were most important to the group? The recorder should be prepared to share one with the whole group.
9.	Recorder: Turn in your team's written statement to the principal. If you are working as a team, your statement will be reformatted and returned to the team for final approval.
10.	If you are working as a whole faculty in small groups, turn your final product in to the principal (who will compile the recommendations and submit them for your final approval).

Visit **go.solution-tree.com/literacy** *to download and print this figure.*

is a problem-solving process developed by Kurt Lewin (1947). Together with your literacy team, you should identify a problem that needs to be solved. During the process, your teachers will then describe the driving forces that will push toward a solution to the problem and the restraining forces that will work against solving the problem.

Force Field Analysis is most effective when it involves the teachers who are most resistant to change and enlists them in solving the problems. The process works well with from five to thirty-five teachers. The most important decision you make in preparation for this process is whether to work with grade-level teams or to mix up the faculty into cross grade-level groups. If you have several teacher teams that border on toxic because they are over-loaded with dysfunctional teachers, divide and conquer. Each small group should have no more than one dysfunctional teacher to provide balance and a generally positive outcome. The directions for the process are as follows. You can facilitate this process yourself or ask a teacher leader to take over.

1. Put a copy of the Force Field Analysis worksheet (figure 4.7, page 90) on an overhead transparency or chart paper. Generate a list of facilitating (positive or driving) forces that will help the team solve

the problem. Answer the question: what forces will help us make the needed change? If a force appears to be complex, break it down into its separate components, if possible. Do not worry at this point about which forces are more important.

2. Generate a list of restraining (negative) forces (include as many as you can think of) that will get in the way of a solution or achievement of a goal. Answer the question: what forces will try to stop change from occurring?

3. Rank the restraining forces, agreeing on two or three that are most important. Rate these for their solvability. Do not waste time focusing on unsolvable problems or "unalterable variables," as they are called by Benjamin Bloom (1980).

4. For each restraining force you have listed as important, describe some possible action steps you might be able to carry out that would reduce the effect of the force or eliminate it completely.

5. Review the action steps you have listed, circle those you intend to do, and move to an action plan immediately, or you may defer that to another meeting.

Figure 4.7: Force Field Analysis Worksheet

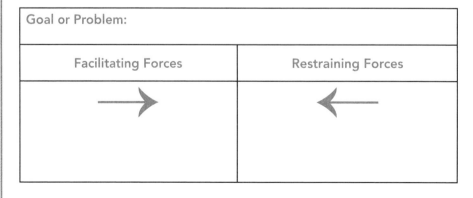

Directions: *Write the goal you are trying to reach or the problem you are trying to solve. Generate a list of facilitating (positive or driving) forces that will help your team or whole school faculty solve the problem or reach the goal. Answer the question: what forces will help us to make the needed change? If a force appears to be complex, break it down into its separate components, if possible. Then generate a list of restraining (negative) forces that will get in the way of a solution or achievement of a goal.*

Goal or Problem:	
Facilitating Forces	Restraining Forces
→	←

*Visit **go.solution-tree.com/literacy** to download and print this figure.*

The Next Step

Now that you have oriented your faculty and they are beginning to think and talk about the literacy look-fors, it's time to begin your first month of classroom walkthroughs to collect frequency data on the look-fors your faculty selected. Chapter 5 will explain that process, and once you have collected your data, you will find directions for aggregating and analyzing it.

Chapter 5

Collect and Analyze Look-For Frequency Data

One of the most powerful aspects of walkthroughs is aggregating data across teachers and over time.

—Pitler & Goodwin (2008, p. 11)

1. Understand the literacy look-fors.

2. Understand the classroom walkthroughs.

3. Assess your instructional leadership capacity.

4. Orient your faculty to the look-fors and walkthroughs.

5. **Collect and analyze look-for frequency data.**

6. Develop, implement, and assess embedded professional development.

7. Use team walkthroughs to build school capacity.

You are ready to take a major step in your implementation of the look-fors and walkthroughs: collecting, aggregating, and analyzing frequency data from classroom walkthroughs. Remember, the purpose of classroom walkthroughs is to aggregate frequency data on various literacy look-fors across grade levels and over time to track the growth of your school's instructional capacity. Just ahead we describe the steps for data collection, aggregation, and analysis. Then we will see how two principals use this process to arrive at a baseline snapshot of their schools' instructional capacity.

Understanding the Data Collection Process

The major benefit of collecting, aggregating, and analyzing walkthrough frequency data during a one-month collection period is that the data reveal trends about instruction, curricula, and professional development of which you and your teachers may be completely unaware. Trend data aggregated from a month-long round of classroom walkthroughs give you and your staff the big picture of instructional capacity that is unavailable from any other source. In anticipation of beginning your classroom walkthroughs, let's briefly review the three components of the data collection process: (1) *collecting*—going out into classrooms with your pilot observation protocol to look for the indicators of effective literacy instruction over teachers and over time, (2) *aggregating*—summing up the look-for frequencies, and (3) *analyzing*—rank ordering the frequencies and scrutinizing them from different perspectives. You want to make sure you don't overlook anything the data might have to reveal to you.

You will use a checksheet—one of the seven basic quality tools developed by the father of quality circles, Kaoru Ishikawa—to collect your data (1985). It is the simplest of the seven quality tools and perfectly suited to our task. Quality-control experts recommend the checksheet procedure when data can be observed and collected repeatedly by the same person or at the same location and when collecting data on the frequency of events (Tague, 2004). In the case of the literacy look-fors, an "event" is an instance in a classroom when the principal observes one of the look-fors. Since data are not collected on individual teachers, all of the tallying for each one-month collection period can be recorded on one, or at the most two (if you run out of room for your tallies) 8 1/2 × 11 data aggregation checksheets. Figure 5.1 is a blank data aggregation checksheet. Using a simple set of frequencies, you are going to use what scientists call a heuristic or basic problem-solving process to analyze your data. Your grandmother called this process "common sense." You may wonder in this day of research-based reading instruction and evidence-based decision making if your own common sense is really enough to inform literacy instruction and decision making in your school. However, even Ian Ayres (2007), author of *Super Crunchers: Why Thinking-by-Numbers Is the New Way to Be Smart*, concedes that intuition has a role to play in the decision-making process, particularly when your walkthroughs will be anchored by sixty research-based indicators.

Assessing Instructional Capacity in a Very Good School

During the writing process, I invited several principals to comment on my early draft of the literacy look-fors observation protocol. A private school

Figure 5.1: Data Aggregation Checksheet

Directions: *Write the look-fors you plan to observe in column 1. Make tally marks in column 2 each time you see the look-for in an individual classroom during a walkthrough. Use a different ink color for each of the four weeks. At the end of the one-month period, count up the tally marks in column 2 and write the total for each row in column 3. Then rank-order the look-fors from high to low by frequency count in column 4, and write each look-for's frequency count in column 5. Finally, calculate the percentage of observations using the total possible occurrences (number of teachers x number of classroom visits) as the divisor and the actual number of occurrences as the dividend; write that number in column 6.*

Data Collection			Data Analysis		
(1) Look-For	(2) Tally of Occurrences During Walk-throughs	(3) Monthly Total	(4) Look-For Frequency: Rank High to Low	(5) Total by Look-For	(6) Percentage Implemen-tation of Look-For

Visit **go.solution-tree.com/literacy** *to download and print this figure.*

principal who wishes to remain anonymous expressed an immediate interest in using the look-fors to structure her classroom walkthroughs. Marlene Mansfield (a pseudonym) had been encouraged by her superintendent to get out of her office and into the classrooms of her school on a more regular basis. However, without anything specific to look for, she felt that her visits were more like social calls than walkthroughs focused on research-based indicators that impacted student learning. While achievement in her school was high, recent pressure to raise it even higher to remain competitive with other private schools in the area had her wondering how she could use her classroom visits to focus on more effective instruction.

Marlene decided that since using the look-fors was an experiment for her to assess her own observation skills in the classroom and not part of any overall plan on her part, she would not share the list of look-fors with her faculty. She did, however, tell them about her personal goal to visit classrooms more frequently and also put them on notice that several items from a recently adopted protocol from corporate headquarters (essential questions, vocabulary, word walls, and the display of outstanding school work) would be on the list of look-fors as requested by her supervisor. Before Marlene began her data collection, I visited her school and walked through every classroom with her using the checksheet. Afterward we debriefed and compared the look-fors we had observed.

Marlene was an alternatively certified administrator who had no actual classroom teaching experience, and although she was skilled at the gestalt of teacher observation (an effective teacher versus an ineffective teacher), she lacked the vocabulary to discuss instruction and the confidence that comes from personal classroom teaching experience. As we compared our frequency counts, finding a high level of congruence, Marlene began to open up about her need to have something substantial she could hold on to in terms of her walkthroughs. The literacy look-fors observation protocol was perfect for her. Over a one-month period, she made one two- to three-minute classroom visit per week to each of her twenty-two preK–4 classrooms, for a total of eighty-eight visits. Figure 5.2 summarizes Marlene's walkthrough data. The only things missing from the figure are Marlene's tally marks. Column 4 contains a rank ordering of the twenty-six look-fors Marlene used. Column 5 contains the number of times Marlene observed a particular look-for out of the eighty-eight opportunities she had to see it, and column 6 displays the percentage of occurrences for a particular look-for.

Figure 5.2: Data Aggregation Checksheet: Desert Springs School

(1) Look-For	(2) Tally of Occurrences During Walk-throughs	(3) Monthly Total	(4) Look-For Frequency: Rank High to Low	(5) Total by Look-For	(6) Percentage Implemen-tation of Look-For
Explaining		76	Outstanding Work	84	95
Giving Directions		56	Vocabulary	83	94
Modeling		36	Essential Questions	83	94
Reminding		28	Student Engagement	82	93
Guiding Practice		43	Explaining	76	86
Scaffolding		7	Word Wall	66	75
Coaching		48	Giving Directions	56	63
Attributing		2	Affirming	55	62
Constructing Meaning		8	Coaching	48	54
Motivating-Connecting		9	Daily Agenda	46	52
Recapping		6	Guiding Practice	43	49
Annotating		6	Assessing	39	44
Assessing		30	Modeling	36	41
Facilitating		13	Organizational Routine	35	40
Redirecting		17	Reminding	28	32
Affirming		55	Academic Routine	25	28
Organizational Routines		35	Redirecting	17	19
Academic Routines		25	Rules	16	18
Social Routines		6	Facilitating	13	15
Essential Question		83	Motivating-Connecting	9	10
Rules		82	Constructing Meaning	8	9
Student Engagement		82	Scaffolding	7	8
Vocabulary		83	Recapping	6	7
Outstanding Work		84	Annotating	6	7
Word Walls		66	Social Routines	6	7
Daily Agenda		46	Attributing	2	2

Recall that we are using common sense and a bit of intuition as we consider what the rank order and various percentages might indicate in terms of school capacity and the need for professional development. In a rank ordering of frequency data such as those found in column 6 of figure 5.2, the most meaningful data can usually be seen on "the tails," the group of look-fors with the highest frequency counts and the group with the lowest. For example, as you consider the look-fors that were observed between 93 and 95 percent of the time, the likelihood of Marlene observing essential questions and vocabulary on the whiteboards in 94 percent of her classroom visits, as a matter of chance, is virtually impossible. If I had not known in advance about the recent administrative mandate regarding the display of student work, content vocabulary, and essential questions, I might have wondered about such high frequency counts for these particular artifacts. The conclusion we can make from these counts is that the majority of Marlene's teachers have complied with the administrative mandate. My question for Marlene related to the likelihood that teachers were indeed integrating these artifacts into daily instruction through a skilled use of particular teaching moves. The high frequency count for explaining indicated to me that teachers were probably spending a fair amount of time talking with students about the importance of the essential question and what students needed to be doing during the lesson to come up with some possible answers for it. However, Marlene's experience brings up an important consideration as you look for the occurrence of artifacts: does the presence of a specific artifact indicate a teacher's *use* of the artifact to increase student learning, or does it merely indicate *compliance*, without building connections to students learning?

Another high frequency count occurred for *student engagement*. Marlene and I spent some time talking about what student engagement indicated on her campus, a pricey private school where parental expectations are very high. Marlene explained that this was going to be one of her assignments during the coming year: to move teachers from being satisfied when students are kept busy with lower-level lessons and activities to challenging more students to expertly apply skills and strategies in new settings and to independently manage and complete a wide range of literacy tasks (including reading, writing, presenting, and consulting). Marlene conceded that when students were "busy" or paying attention to the teacher when she visited, she likely counted that as an occurrence of student engagement. Shifting teachers' paradigms from one definition of student engagement to true academic engagement will require some embedded professional development. Marlene's experience highlights the value of finding an administrative partner, literacy coach, or small leadership team with whom to talk about the frequency data. Staff members who work with many teachers in the building and are in and out of classrooms frequently can bring another perspective to your frequency findings.

Marlene was particularly concerned about the low frequency for scaffolding. There are several things we might conclude about this low frequency count: (1) the teachers were scaffolding, but Marlene didn't recognize it, (2) almost none of the teachers were scaffolding, or (3) the teachers and Marlene are working with different operational definitions of the term *scaffolding*. Marlene assured me that she was diligently looking for scaffolding during her walkthroughs and could honestly say that she never saw it being employed in more than a couple of classrooms. A large number of her teachers had attended a conference specifically to acquire strategies for scaffolding struggling students in large-group instruction. She said it was a topic that everybody talked about, including her, but obviously, talking about this critical instructional move hadn't translated into action in the classrooms. The "talking about" scaffolding could have been superficial, without relevance to actual lessons and students. It may be that in order to actually implement scaffolding in their classrooms, Marlene's teachers need to go deeper, considering examples and nonexamples of this instructional move and, if possible, walking through some classrooms to see their colleagues using scaffolding. I suggested a book for Marlene's upper-grade teachers, *Scaffolding Student Learning* (Hogan & Pressley, 1997), that unpacks scaffolding in a way that would benefit the strong students in Marlene's school who are not being sufficiently challenged in their critical thinking skills. Marlene was also concerned about why she did not see more *attributing* during instruction and noted it for discussion with her instructional coach.

Are We Really Teaching Reading Comprehension?

Bob Stephens has been the principal of Greentree School for five years. [Note: Bob Stephens, Greentree School, and the frequency data are composites of several schools.] Although Bob and his staff have made some incremental progress in raising literacy standards in Greentree's primary grades, Bob is concerned about reading comprehension instruction, particularly in the upper grades. His teachers regularly reassure him that they are teaching comprehension every day, but their instruction is not producing results on the school's yearly summative test. Bob does a lot of professional reading and recently read statements from several experts about a fairly widespread lack of comprehension instruction in schools generally. He would like to reverse that trend at Greentree. Here are the statements he read.

> It is not clear to what extent teachers actually teach children the [comprehension] strategies that have proven effective in experimental and quasi-experimental studies. Observations of teachers in naturalistic settings suggest that they do not spend significant amounts of time explicitly teaching students how to comprehend what they are reading. (Connor, Morrison, & Petrella, 2004, p. 682)

> Despite a significant body of research in the 1980s suggesting the effectiveness of strategy instruction, especially for lower-achieving readers, strategy instruction has not been implemented in many American classrooms. (Dole, 2000, p. 62)

> Most teachers offered little useful instruction in how to read for meaning. (Allington, 2001, p. 21)

> Despite research establishing the effectiveness of instruction designed to enhance comprehension, typical classrooms across primary and upper elementary grades do not devote adequate time and attention to comprehension instruction. (Snow, 2002, p. 43)

A sizable percentage of Greentree's students are not reaching proficient levels on the state assessment, and many more are not even making basic levels. The teachers have identified five possible reasons for the low achievement: (1) the reading curriculum, (2) the fact that students don't voluntarily read enough, (3) the parents' lack of support for the school's reading incentive programs, (4) the amount of time students spend watching TV and playing computer games, and (5) students' short attention spans. Bob concedes that some of these reasons may contribute to the problem, but he is also aware that his teachers did not mention the quality or quantity of their own comprehension instruction as a possible reason for low comprehension scores.

Bob decides to develop a customized set of literacy look-fors (see figure 5.3) focused on the direct instruction of reading comprehension strategies to collect his baseline data. Bob has been reviewing these descriptions in anticipation of beginning his search for comprehension instruction at Greentree. Note that the data aggregation checksheet Bob prepares does not contain any definitions in order to provide space for the tally marks he will make as he sees various look-fors. He takes care to list the look-fors on the checksheet in the same order as they appear on the protocol to make it easier to recall the definitions he has been studying, and he decides to take a copy of figure 5.3 on his walkthroughs to occasionally confirm a definition. He finds a set of pens in four different colors of ink, one for each week of data collection.

During the first week, he will make his tally marks on the data aggregation checksheet in red. During the second week, he will use another color. Bob also decides that since he is interrupted so frequently during the working day and may need to double up on his walkthroughs on another day, he will keep track of the teachers he visits on a copy of his faculty roster. He asks his secretary to prepare one for him with four columns. He will use one per week to make sure that he walks through every classroom every week. Once he finds a clipboard in the supply closet, he will be ready to head out on Monday morning.

Figure 5.3: Observation Protocol—Directly Instructing Reading Comprehension Strategies

Category	Description of the Literacy Look-For
Teacher-Managed Instructional Activity	**Directly Teaching Reading Comprehension** As appropriate to the assessed needs of students, the teacher directly teaches reading comprehension using the instructional moves noted as appropriate.
Student-Managed Learning Activity	**Student Application of Cognitive Strategies In Grade-Level or Above Text** As appropriate to assessed independent reading levels, students are able to successfully apply appropriate cognitive strategies to extract and construct meaning from text in the context of reading in the classroom.
Instructional Move	**Directly Instructing** The teacher directly teaches and works face to face with students using a systematic and explicit approach to teaching each cognitive strategy that includes describing the critical attributes of the strategy and providing concrete examples and nonexamples of the strategy.
Instructional Move	**Explaining** The teacher explains the purpose of the cognitive strategy and how it serves the student during the act of reading. The teacher tells students what will happen during a cognitive strategy lesson, what the goals are, why it's important, how it will help students, and what the roles of the teacher and student will be during the lesson.
Instructional Move	**Coaching-Facilitating** The teacher coaches students in the use of a particular strategy by asking them to think-aloud about their cognitive processing and cueing them to choose strategies that have been previously taught.

continued →

Category	Description of the Literacy Look-For
Instructional Move	**Modeling** The teacher specifically thinks aloud for students regarding personal cognitive processing (for example, making connections with prior knowledge to something that was read in the text, showing how an inference was made, or demonstrating how to write a summary).
Instructional Move	**Attributing** The teacher communicates to students that their understanding of the text is the result of effort, wise decision making about what strategies to use, attending to the task, exercising good judgment, and perseverance, *rather* than their intelligence or making a "good guess."
Instructional Move	**Constructing** The teacher and students work collaboratively to construct multiple meanings from conversations, discussions, and the reading together of text.
Instructional Move	**Recapping** The teacher summarizes what has been concluded, learned, or constructed during a given comprehension lesson or discussion and tells students why this new learning is important and where it can be applied and connected in the future.
Instructional Move	**Differentiating** The teacher calibrates and manipulates the difficulty levels of tasks so as to create the best match between the learner and the task, avoiding whenever possible the "too easy for some" tasks that create boredom and disinterest, and the "too hard for some" tasks that create fear and avoidance. This kind of calibration in terms of text difficulty is critical when teaching cognitive strategies in which large amounts of working memory are needed to understand and apply the strategies during reading. Text that is too difficult will reduce the possibility that students will acquire the strategy being taught.
Instructional Move	**Scaffolding** The teacher provides instructional support within students' zones of proximal development (the difference between students' independent performance levels on progressively more complex tasks, and their potential performance levels).
Classroom Artifacts	**Charts** Charts containing steps or prompts to scaffold students' use of cognitive strategies.

*Visit **go.solution-tree.com/literacy** to download and print this figure.*

Greentree School has thirty K–5 classrooms, and Bob is the only administrator. Conducting walkthroughs in all of his classrooms every week sounded time consuming, but Bob is surprised when he does the math. He has thirty K–5 classrooms and plans to make four walkthroughs per classroom (a once-per-week walkthrough for each teacher) during the one-month period. This translates into each teacher having four opportunities to be "caught" teaching reading comprehension during the month. He computes that the collective faculty has 120 opportunities to be caught teaching reading comprehension during the month. Bob further calculates that if he spends three minutes in each classroom, the walkthroughs will consume no more than eighteen minutes per day: 30 teachers × 4 walkthroughs × 3 minutes per walkthrough = 360 minutes per month / 20 instructional days = 18 minutes per day. If he can become more skilled at identifying the look-fors, he can cut his time to two minutes per walkthrough. Bob calculates that the time required daily will drop to only twelve minutes: 30 teachers × 4 walkthroughs × 2 minutes = 240 minutes per month / 20 instructional days = 12 minutes per day.

Bob finds it to be a reasonable assumption that if anybody out there is teaching comprehension at all, he will find it during his classroom walkthroughs. Although Bob does not give the protocol to his faculty since he is collecting baseline data, he does announce in his Monday bulletin that he will be in every classroom during the week looking for reading comprehension instruction. He assures the teachers who ask him that he is not collecting information for teacher evaluations and readily shows his staff the checksheet he is using to collect the data. After Bob completes his one-month data collection, aggregating the data is fairly simple. Greentree's data is displayed in figure 5.4 (page 104). For each of the look-fors in his protocol, he counts the number of tally marks in the column labeled "Tally of Occurrences During Walkthroughs" and writes that number under the corresponding column. He then rank orders his list of look-fors from the highest frequency count to lowest in column 5 and calculates the percentages for column 6 using the 120 observations as the divisor and each frequency count as the dividend.

Bob's findings are disappointing to him, but certainly not surprising. As he examines the range of frequency counts, he finds that his teachers are doing more "coaching" of students while they are reading than anything else on his protocol—*encouraging students to think aloud and choose the right strategies while they were reading in their guided reading groups.* Teachers seldom (if ever) actually taught students the strategies that they were coaching. It reminded Bob of the football coach who never directly instructs his players in the moves to make for each of the complicated plays he will call during the Saturday game. He expects his players to catch on by hanging around the practice field. Bob wants to find evidence that his teachers are directly instructing cognitive strategies, but it just isn't there.

Figure 5.4: Data Aggregation Checksheet for Greentree School

(1) Look-For	(2) Tally of Occurrences During Walk-throughs	(3) Monthly Total	(4) Look-For Frequency: Rank High to Low	(5) Total by Look-For	(6) Percentage Implementation of Look-For
Directly Teaching Comprehension	✱✱✱✱ ||||	9	Coaching	65	54
Students Applying Cognitive Strategies	✱✱✱✱	5	Constructing Meaning	19	16
Directly Instructing	✱✱✱✱ ✱✱✱✱	10	Modeling	13	11
Explaining	✱✱✱✱ ||	7	Directly Instructing	10	8
Coaching	✱✱✱✱ ✱✱✱✱ ✱✱✱✱ ✱✱✱✱ ✱✱✱✱ ✱✱✱✱ ✱✱✱✱ ✱✱✱✱ ✱✱✱✱ ✱✱✱✱ ✱✱✱✱ ✱✱✱✱ ✱✱✱✱	65	Scaffolding	10	8
Modeling	✱✱✱✱ ✱✱✱✱ |||	13	Teacher-Managed Comprehension	9	7
Attributing	✱✱✱✱	5	Recapping	7	6
Constructing Meaning	✱✱✱✱ ✱✱✱✱ ✱✱✱✱ ||||	19	Explaining	7	6
Recapping	✱✱✱✱ ||	7	Student-Managed Comprehension	5	4
Targeting	✱✱✱✱	5	Targeting	5	4
Scaffolding	✱✱✱✱ ✱✱	10	Attributing	5	4
Cognitive Strategy Charts	|||	3	Cognitive Strategy Charts	3	3

Even more disappointing than the fact that his teachers weren't teaching reading comprehension was the fact that during guided reading groups, he noticed that many students were unable to answer teachers' factual comprehension questions—more evidence of a lack of comprehension instruction. Another disturbing thing he noticed (not on his list of look-fors) was the level of questionable activity taking place during the literacy block, at both upper and lower grades. Upper-grade students were ostensibly working on PowerPoint programs for reports, but could not articulate the objective of the assignment and did not have a rubric to communicate how they would be evaluated; lower-grade students were engaged in art projects. To their credit, teachers directly taught word identification skills, vocabulary, and fluency, but Bob tallied only nine instances of teachers explaining and directly instructing students in the seven cognitive strategies of highly effective readers and only thirteen instances of teachers modeling their personal cognitive processing by thinking aloud for students.

As he reflects on the data, Bob does feel a measure of excitement. He has addressed the issue of comprehension instruction in the past, but without data, he felt he lacked the leverage he needed. There are so many ways for educators to avoid accountability: the test, the kids, the time of year, the curriculum, the budget, and so on. However, Bob's frequency data regarding comprehension instruction gives him a new variable to add to the list of reasons why comprehension is so low: lack of comprehension instruction. He plans to install some embedded professional development in his collaborative grade-level teams as soon as he can gather the necessary resources.

Managing Your Energy for What's Important

One of the questions principals frequently raise regarding classroom walk-throughs is how they will be able to find the time to go on classroom walk-throughs. You will only spend between eight and sixteen minutes for a two-minute walkthrough and twelve to twenty-four minutes for a three-minute walkthrough, even if you have as many as forty teachers on your walkthrough schedule. This means that you will have ample time to visit classrooms for other reasons:

- ❑ Conducting teacher evaluation observations that are part of the district's plan
- ❑ Monitoring, supervising, and evaluating new teachers
- ❑ Visiting classrooms of struggling teachers who need to know you are there and that you are monitoring their teaching effectiveness

❑ Monitoring and supervising troubled teachers with anger issues or inappropriate behavior with students

❑ Observing individual students in preparation for a child study team meeting or a staffing

❑ Monitoring the implementation of new curriculum

❑ Responding to invitations from teachers to visit their classrooms

Where did we ever get the idea that principals could and should visit every classroom in their schools every day? I can't document where the notion came from, but I have been as guilty as anyone of perpetuating it, simply because it seemed like an important thing to do. However, it is an unrealistic expectation, and the sooner you let go of it, the more energy you will have to undertake the essential classroom visits. I think you will agree that when you add up the time needed for the daily classroom walkthroughs to collect frequency data, formal observations for teacher evaluation, supervision and monitoring of new, difficult, or marginal teachers, and curricular supervision for new program implementation, you do not have time left for going to every classroom every day just to hang around and say hello. Of course, it makes you feel good and somewhat justifies not doing the critical things that need to be done for monitoring program implementation. You might be able to carve out time for this kind of walkthrough if you have a team of assistants and a literacy coach or two to assist you. However, that is not the norm in elementary schools. This is one reason that I do not recommend writing feedback notes to teachers after classroom walkthroughs. You simply do not have enough data to give quality feedback to a teacher based on a two-minute visit. Consequently, this activity ends up sapping your energy and creating stress because there is not enough time to do it right.

Instead, I recommend that you make regular visits to collaborative teacher team meetings to support and encourage them as a unit. If you are feeling guilty about not affirming your "star" teachers more frequently, take teacher teams on walkthroughs through their classrooms to illustrate various look-fors. Or ask these stars to teach sample lessons in faculty meetings. Stretch their leadership capacities, and they will not only grow as individuals, but they will begin to grow the collective capacity of your school.

The Next Step

Customizing professional development is next on the agenda. In chapter 6 you will listen in as principals and teachers wrestle with using the look-fors to engage in professional development activities that contribute to student learning and achievement.

Chapter 6

Develop, Implement, and Assess Embedded Professional Development

Changes in schools may be initiated from without, but the most important and lasting change will come from within.

—Barth (1990, p. 159)

1. Understand the literacy look-fors.

2. Understand the classroom walkthroughs.

3. Assess your instructional leadership capacity.

4. Orient your faculty to the look-fors and walkthroughs.

5. Collect and analyze look-for frequency data.

6. **Develop, implement, and assess embedded professional development.**

7. Use team walkthroughs to build school capacity.

If you have been diligently climbing the seven steps to a power-packed implementation of the literacy look-fors and walkthroughs, you have just finished collecting, aggregating, and analyzing the data from your first round of walkthroughs. Put the final data analysis in a safe place. You will want to compare your frequency counts from this baseline data collection with the frequency counts you obtain after your staff has engaged in the embedded professional development described in this chapter.

Your goal in this chapter is to move your faculty to an embedded professional development model, a delivery system that speaks directly to the achievement challenges of your school (your students' needs) and the instructional profiles of your teachers (your teachers' needs). There will always be a need for whole-group professional development in the library or some off-site district-provided program, but embedded professional development will hold your teachers to a much higher standard. Embedded professional development almost guarantees (once fully underway) that every team member will participate and be accountable, not only to their team members but also to other grade-level teams and the principal. Embedded professional development for collaborative teacher teams addresses problems that frequently cannot be addressed by generic professional development:

❏ How can collaborative grade-level teams become more effective in increasing literacy learning and achievement?

❏ How can grade-level teams design and deliver instruction that targets exactly what struggling students need to gain literacy proficiency?

❏ How can grade-level teams organize their classrooms more efficiently to increase interactive teaching time for all students whether average, struggling, or accelerated?

❏ How can grade-level teams teach their students to become more self-directed and motivated?

The following six phases of implementation are critical to success. The goal in this step is to demonstrate to your staff the power of collaborative learning that connects their professional growth to their students' learning.

The Phases of Step 6

Recall from the Suggested Implementation Timeline we established in the introduction (figure I.3, page 9), that Step 6 has six phases that will extend over two and a half to three months (depending on how frequently your collaborative teams are able to meet to work on their professional development assignment).

❏ Phase 6a—Share the results of frequency data collection with your literacy team, and select the literacy look-for that will be the focus of embedded professional development.

❏ Phase 6b—Share the results of frequency data collection with teachers, and identify the look-for selected by the literacy team.

❏ Phase 6c—Model the look-for unpacking process for faculty, and describe the summarizing activity to take place after implementation.

❑ Phase 6d—Hold a meeting to hear the summarizing presentations from each team.

❑ Phase 6e—Facilitate the development of student achievement goals at each grade level, and set a date (twenty student attendance days from the beginning date) to report on the goal achievement.

❑ Phase 6f—Engage in a follow-up frequency data collection to determine the effectiveness of the embedded professional development combined and the student achievement goals.

Pay close attention to the following more detailed descriptions of the six phases of Step 6. Each one holds potential challenges. Be prepared to have assertive conversations with team members who are totally frustrated with the project. Coach and facilitate teams that are stuck because they have not yet learned to work together or are finding the assignment too open-ended or difficult. However, never give any individual teacher or team the idea that the assignment is negotiable. Your faculty must know that you are confident and will see this implementation through to the end.

Phase 6a: Share Information with Your Leadership Team

If you have not already formed an advisory literacy leadership team, invite your literacy coach, Title I and special education teachers, grade-level team leaders, and specialists (such as the school psychologist and speech-language pathologist or some subset of this group), and discuss the frequency data and your preliminary analysis. Share the look-for that emerged as the obvious first choice for embedded professional development. If needed, review the process described in chapter 5 for selecting the look-for around which to build your first embedded professional development experience for teachers.

Phase 6b: Share Information with Teachers

Phase 6b is a short but important part of the process: sharing the results of your month-long set of classroom walkthroughs with your faculty. If you didn't prepare PowerPoint slides for your presentation to the literacy team, prepare a PowerPoint presentation that explains what you found, not in individual classrooms or individual grade levels but across *all* teachers in the school. Remind them that you did not collate the data by individual classrooms or by grade levels and that your focus is on building instructional capacity collectively. Recall the Affinity Process you and your faculty used to select the four look-fors on your pilot observation protocol. Ask the faculty if they can infer any connections between what happened during that process and the findings from the walkthroughs. Give teams time to discuss this question, and invite a reporter from each team to share their observations.

There is no way to predict what your findings will be or how your staff will respond to the findings. However, you can be assured that presenting frequency data to staff will be far less stressful (for you and them) than presenting test scores grade by grade or classroom by classroom. Remember that the frequency data is a snapshot of the collective faculty over a one-month time span and represents the instructional capacity of the school for implementing a selected look-for. Emphasize the power of collective instructional capacity along with joint accountability and responsibility for ensuring that all students succeed. Continue to remind your faculty of the power of collective instructional capacity.

Phase 6c: Model the Unpacking Process

Teachers will need a second packet of handouts for Phase 6c. They were not included in the orientation handout, but are listed in figure 6.1 and are available for download at **go.solution-tree.com/literacy**.

Figure 6.1: Table of Contents for Unpacking a Look-For Handout

Title of Handout	Figure Number and Page Number	Purpose
Unpacking a Literacy Look-For	Figure 6.2, p. 113	This figure provides a narrative description of the unpacking process and is based on the metaphor of packing and unpacking belongings for a move.
A Step-by-Step Approach to Unpacking a Literacy Look-For	Figure 6.3, p. 114	This figure provides step-by-step instructions for the unpacking process.
Modeling the Unpacking of a Literacy Look-For	Figure 6.4, p. 115	This figure is a narrative description of a literacy coach modeling the unpacking process.
Unpacking Directly Instructing Research-Based Presentation Techniques for Teaching Discrete Skills	Figure 6.5, p. 116	This figure contains a set of "little look-fors" that the literacy coach unpacked in her modeling narrative in figure 6.4.

Title of Handout	Figure Number and Page Number	Purpose
A Lesson Template for Directly Teaching a Cognitive Strategy	Figure 6.6, p. 117	This figure illustrates another way to unpack the directly instructing literacy look-for.
Teacher Team Goal-Setting Worksheet	Figure 6.7, p. 119	This figure is used by teacher teams as they set achievement goals for students after they engage in embedded professional development.
Teacher Team Action Log	Figure 6.8, p. 120	This is an optional figure to be used by a teacher team in conjunction with implementing the team's achievement goal.

Before you tackle how to unpack a look-for and model it for your teachers, recall this statement from the preface: the data you collect during your walkthroughs can guide your selection of professional resources, dictate the types of whole-school professional growth activities you plan, and inform the budget you build to foster professional growth in your staff, but in reality the sixty look-fors are only an appetizer for what I hope will be a gourmet adventure of literacy learning for you and your staff. Step 6 in the implementation is where your "gourmet adventure" begins. And guess who is stirring things up, "Chef Principal"?

Let me explain. I have been working with the literacy look-fors observation protocol in one form or another for more than a decade. The sixty look-fors seem straightforward enough, but they are deceptive in their simplicity. Each of the five categories contains enough material for a book. I know this because I've written six books (McEwan, 1998, 2002b, 2004, 2006, 2009b; McEwan-Adkins, 2010) that include one or more of the look-for categories. And there are hundreds of books written by other teachers, principals, staff developers, and professors that provide in-depth treatments of literacy instruction from their unique perspectives.

Furthermore, each look-for contains an idea or concept that is deep and wide enough to consume any academic scholar for a lifetime. You have encountered dozens of citations containing the names of individuals who have devoted their careers to finding answers and then sharing with teachers just what works in literacy classrooms. How then are you, your literacy team, and your teachers going to make sense of all of this so it translates into learning for the students in your school?

The answer to that question is one step at a time. Begin where the need is the greatest, with the look-for from your pilot look-for observation protocol that came up "missing" in more classrooms of your school than any other—the one that you and your team have just selected to be the focus of your teachers' embedded professional development. Your grade-level teams are going to unpack this look-for, take it apart, put it back together in new ways, read about it, write about it, discuss it, and even disagree about it. They will design lessons integrating the look-for and eventually decide how they are going to implement this look-for in their classrooms in a way that will impact their students' learning. Your teachers will become experts at implementing this particular look-for. They will need some resource materials to accomplish that goal: handouts that you will provide for them and as many resources as they can locate on the Internet, in your professional library, and in the references of this book.

Figure 6.2 describes the unpacking process using the metaphor of packing and unpacking for a move. Faculty members will have copies of this figure to read as they engage in the unpacking process.

While figure 6.2 may appeal to the more visual and imaginative members of your collaborative grade-level teams, figure 6.3 is designed for teachers who crave step-by-step instructions. Together the two figures provide enough to get your faculty started on their unpacking process. In addition to these handouts, team members will have to find resources in the school's professional library, their own personal professional libraries, and the Internet. The step-by-step approach in figure 6.3 is meant to be suggestive rather than literal. Once the team gets going, members will undoubtedly discover other steps unique to their team's unpacking and go far beyond the instructions in the figure.

The challenge of modeling the unpacking process is that the minute you give teachers an example, they will want to know where they can find one just like it for the look-for they will be unpacking. For this particular exercise, the process is more important than the product. Encourage your teachers to search the Internet and professional library, selecting ideas and concepts that seem relevant to their look-for and building their own version (mental model or concept map) of the unpacked look-for. If you have the budget, offer to buy one or two books of a team's choosing to help them in the study. Focus particularly on books found in the references section of this book.

Figure 6.2: Unpacking a Literacy Look-For

The unpacking process is not as mysterious as it may sound. Here is an example to help you understand what it looks like. Imagine that with very little notice you were offered a two-year assignment to teach in Egypt. You had no time to pack up your apartment, so friends and family members packed your belongings for you. Although they tried to keep things organized and labeled, as time grew short they simply grabbed whatever was left, wrapped it in old towels or newsprint, and stuffed it in a box they labeled "miscellaneous." Belongings that you once used on a daily basis were put into storage.

Now, fast-forward to your return from Egypt. You have had a fabulous experience, but after a two-year separation from your belongings, it's time to move into a new apartment and get settled. The unpacking you do at that moment is most comparable to the conceptual unpacking of an instructional move. Let me further explain the similarities between the two processes.

Unpacking a literacy look-for that seems fairly straightforward at first glance is like tearing open the miscellaneous box. As you open this mystery box, you have no idea what you will find. You know that each item you unwrap belongs to you, but somehow as you hold each item in your hand, you may not even recognize it. Perhaps the object you hold is only one part of a whole—a shoe without its mate or a tangle of cords and chargers separated from their appliances, computers, and cell phones. You have two years of exciting experiences behind you and now are actually wondering if the coffee mug, that piece of art, and an article of clothing that seemed so dear two years earlier are even worth saving now. In the course of your unpacking you will be throwing away things that are no longer relevant and constructing a new life.

The same is true of your team as you collectively unpack a literacy look-for. You and your colleagues may have fuzzy definitions stored in your long-term memories, but as you share them with one another, you discover aspects of the look-for that had never before occurred to you. You realize that a particular look-for needs to be combined with and supported by other look-fors. As you listen to your teammates talk about how they employ various look-fors, you may suddenly realize that your previous understanding of the look-for will have to be discarded in favor of a new, comprehensive, and definitely more research-based version.

The process of unpacking a literacy look-for can be a little messy because it is a cognitive processing exercise in which team members retrieve knowledge, experiences, feelings, and perceptions about teaching and learning from their cognitive and social-emotional memory systems, place this "package" on the desktops of their working memories, and then after some discussion, reconstruct a new "package" of knowledge that they send back to their long-term memories for later retrieval. Your team is co-constructing knowledge. You may find your conceptual thinking begin to shift as you struggle with what implementing a specific look-for means to your students who are failing to survive and thrive in your classrooms.

Visit **go.solution-tree.com/literacy** *to download and print this figure.*

Figure 6.3: A Step-by-Step Approach to Unpacking a Literacy Look-For

1. Gather materials that relate to the look-for from a professional library or the Internet, or purchase materials if budgets permit.	Don't think in terms of reading everything. Do more searching and selecting of interesting ideas, explanations, quotations, and so on. Divide up the reading and jigsaw it, with each team member reporting back on what was read.
2. Rewrite the description of the look-for by putting it into language that is meaningful to you and your colleagues but retains the essence of the original research-based definition.	Unpacking a look-for requires thinking more deeply about an educational concept that is discussed and used with frequency, but that is often not clearly understood by educators (particularly those who are new to the profession).
3. Divide up the materials among the team members, and begin looking for ways in which the look-for could be expanded into more specific teacher behaviors. You can call them "little look-fors" to distinguish them from the "big" look-for that is part of the look-for observation protocol.	You might construct an outline with Roman numerals and subheadings. Or, if you are a more visually oriented team, make a large concept map and put it on the wall of one of the team's classrooms. If you do not wish to post it, roll up the butcher paper on which you are constructing the map and bring it out for each meeting.
4. As you begin to develop an expanded definition of the look-for with as many categories or subheadings as you can find, define all of the related terms and concepts so you and your teammates can achieve consensus about what each term or concept means in terms of implementing with your students.	Always take time to nail down specific definitions and behaviors. Look for research that supports your findings, if needed, to show teammates who are having a hard time letting go of a paradigm that has no research to support it.
5. Brainstorm as many "little look-fors" as you can that could be used as subheadings in your outline.	Write down as many ideas as you can think of without regard for correctness. You can always trim the list later.
6. Begin to construct classroom examples and nonexamples of the "little look-fors."	Start with the question, "What does a good one look like?" Think of your answer as the exemplar of teacher effectiveness on the far left of a continuum. Then move to the far right of the continuum and ask, "What does an unacceptable version of the exemplar look like?" That's your nonexemplar.
8. Talk about how your classrooms would change if you implemented all of the "little look-fors" with automaticity and accuracy.	Focus on struggling students and imagine how your implementation would impact their learning.
9. Think about how you will intentionally use what you have learned about the look-for in your classrooms.	Take notes about all of these suggestions so you can review them, *or* make a reminder poster to hang at the back of the classroom to scaffold your implementation.
10. Set an achievement goal for your students based on your implementation of the literacy look-for.	Student learning is the ultimate goal of embedded professional development. As you are learning about the look-fors, constantly think about making connections to student learning.

Visit **go.solution-tree.com/literacy** *to download and print this figure.*

Figure 6.4 is a narrative description of a literacy coach modeling the unpacking process. It is intended to help you, the principal, think aloud and model the unpacking process. You may or may not include this figure in the set of handouts. No matter how uncomfortable this process makes you, make every effort to do it personally. You can tell your teachers afterward that you are very confident that they will be far more skilled at this process than you have been.

Figure 6.4: Modeling the Unpacking of a Literacy Look-For

The principal explains that to understand and implement a literacy look-for, it's often necessary to have a deeper understanding of it. The principal also explains that gaining that deeper understanding requires that the team engage in a variety of processing activities. The literacy look-for she is unpacking for her brief modeling session is directly instructing, in which the teacher directly teaches or works face to face with students using an explicit and systematic approach. She explains that she knows from her experience that directly instructing can look at least two ways—depending on whether the teacher is teaching a discrete skill, such as blending sounds, or a higher-level thinking skill needed for a cognitive strategy, such as inferring. In addition to her experience, she searched and selected information from several books to help her more clearly understand directly instructing (Bursuck & Blanks, 2010; McEwan, 2006; McEwan, 2009b; McEwan-Adkins, 2010; Bursuck & Damer, 2010).

The principal shares with teachers that in one of the books in the professional library, she found a subset of look-fors that research shows are particularly effective for directly instructing discrete skills such as blending sounds, sound-spelling correspondences, and vocabulary found in new stories. The presentation techniques are research based and very powerful in terms of bringing students to mastery of these discrete skills. The principal goes on to explain (after the teachers have looked over figure 6.5) that unpacking the directly instructing move when it is used to teach the seven cognitive strategies used by highly effective readers requires a different set of look-fors. She has used bold print in the Lesson Template for Directly Teaching a Cognitive Strategy (figure 6.6, page 117) to emphasize them: *explaining*, *modeling*, *guiding practice*, *coaching-facilitating*, and *questioning*. The principal then points out that her exercise of unpacking the directly instructing move has shown her how this move interacts with several other look-fors (the instructional moves of explaining, modeling, guiding practice, coaching-facilitating, and questioning).

In conclusion, the principal shares with the teachers that while she was engaged in the unpacking process in anticipation of this meeting, she arrived at a much deeper understanding of the directly instructing literacy look-for. She had previously only thought in terms of the presentation techniques shown in figure 6.6. Now she has expanded her understanding to include how the directly instructing literacy look-for plays a role in comprehension strategy instruction.

continued →

She reminds the teachers that the unpacking process stimulates reflective thinking and discussion and will help everyone begin to wrap their minds around the very challenging literacy look-for they will be unpacking in their collaborative teams. She offers her assistance to any of the teams that may need her help.

Visit **go.solution-tree.com/literacy** to download and print this figure.

Figure 6.5 is an illustration of how the principal in figure 6.4 unpacked the directly instructing look-for in her presentation to teachers. Recall that citations to the resources the coach used are cited in the Step-by-Step Approach to Unpacking a Literacy Look-For handout (figure 6.3, page 114).

Figure 6.5: Unpacking Directly Instructing Research-Based Presentation Techniques for Teaching Discrete Skills

Systematic Error Correction	The teacher provides immediate corrective feedback to students by modeling the correct answer, guiding students to the correct answer as needed, and then asking the corrected student to give the answer independently. The teacher then uses delayed testing by asking the student to repeat the correct answer later in the lesson.
Judicious Use of Teacher Talk	The teacher presents the lesson in concise statements using language the students are able to understand. The teacher does not present information unrelated to the task the students are to complete or provide verbose explanations, nor does the teacher distract herself (or her students) with comments unrelated to the lesson.
Signaling	The teacher provides a cue alerting students when to make a response. The cue can be visual (pointing to a letter or running hand underneath a word), verbal (saying, "Get ready!"), or auditory (a hand clap or pencil tap). The purpose of signaling is to give all students an opportunity to think about the answer to a question, thereby eliminating the calling out of answers by students who can retrieve answers more quickly.
Wait Time	The teacher provides a thinking pause immediately after giving the directions. It lasts for as many seconds as the teacher feels are needed to give all students a chance to figure out the answer. Without the wait time, more advanced students will shout out the answer.
Brisk Instructional Pace	Keeping a "perky pace" is important to minimize the amount of time between activities and the amount of time between a student's answer and the teacher's next question or prompt. Students need to feel the energy in order to attend.
Motivational Reinforcement	The teacher strengthens appropriate academic and social behaviors by using positive reinforcement. The teacher increases social behaviors (such as students staying in their seats, raising their hands before talking, keeping their hands to themselves,

Motivational Reinforcement *(continued)*	and so on) by delivering consistent praise for these behaviors. The goal is to maintain a 3:1 ratio of praise for appropriate behavior to a correction of criticism for problem behavior. The teacher also delivers reinforcement to peers who are displaying appropriate behavior. For academic behaviors, the teacher adjusts the level of reinforcement to fit the difficulty level of the task.
Cumulative Review and Practice	The teacher maximizes opportunities for practice by increasing the number of practice items and finding additional time during the school day for practice. The cumulative aspect of practice ensures that previously introduced skills are constantly included with new material during practice.
Unison Responses	The teacher signals all students to answer together to maximize practice and regularly monitor student progress. The teacher asks questions of individual students as an additional check of progress only after the whole group is correctly answering all of the questions together.
Individual Checks	After the teacher is assured that all students are answering correctly, he or she will then begin to check in with individual students to see if they can answer the question without the support of the group. If students cannot, the teacher will then go back to unison responding and practice to build confidence and avoid embarrassing students.

Visit go.solution-tree.com/literacy to download and print this figure.

Figure 6.6 is a lesson template for directly instructing a cognitive strategy. It uses several familiar instructional moves, but does not contain any of the presentation techniques shown in figure 6.5. The goal of presenting these two figures during the modeling process is to show teachers that the directly instructing look-for, when unpacked, reveals far more than its definition conveys or that they personally understood the definition to mean.

Figure 6.6: A Lesson Template for Directly Teaching a Cognitive Strategy

	Lesson Notes
1. Provide direct instruction regarding the strategy.	
a. Define and **explain** the cognitive strategy.	
b. **Explain** the purpose the cognitive strategy serves during the act of reading.	
c. Describe the critical attributes of the cognitive strategy.	
d. Provide concrete examples and nonexamples of the strategy.	
2. **Model** the strategy by thinking-aloud for students.	

continued →

	Lesson Notes
3. **Facilitate guided practice** with students.	
4. Follow up by **coaching** and **scaffolding** students' strategy usage through Socratic **questioning**.	

Visit **go.solution-tree.com/literacy** *to download and print this figure.*

During the month-long embedded professional development experience of your grade-level teams, schedule one or two brief visits with each team, depending on the frequency of team meetings. The purpose of these visits is to let the team know that you are holding them accountable, to find out if they are experiencing difficulties with the unpacking process, and to suggest strategies that might get them unstuck. Each team will vary in their approach and progress during this assignment. In addition to sending out a printed memo to teachers about the presentation of their team summarizers at the end of the time you have scheduled for the completion of the embedded professional development project, remind them in person during these visits.

Phase 6d: Present Team Summarizers

When your grade-level teams come together at the end of the month, everyone will have an opportunity to view the various products (graphic organizers, notes, lists of resources they consulted or printed from the Internet, outlines, lesson plans, and so on). Everyone will also be able to hear and see the one-minute presentation that each team has prepared to summarize the look-for. It can be a poem, song, rap, or an elevator speech (a speech one might give during a one-minute elevator ride to tell someone about the main idea of the selected literacy look-for). The elevator speech can also be presented as bullet points.

The goal of this final presentation is to create some team spirit and camaraderie in the teams as well as to bring closure to this first embedded professional development project. Any team that did not take this project seriously during this first round will definitely be motivated by the work of other teams and resolve to expend more cognitive effort on their next assignment.

Phase 6e: Set and Achieve Student Literacy Goals

At the end of their embedded professional development experience, each grade-level team will be ready to set a student literacy goal based on their newly acquired knowledge and skills. Setting short-term team goals engages teachers immediately in using what they have learned during their customized professional development sessions. While teachers may well have been trying out various "little look-fors" during their study (and you hope they have), a formalized goal for which they will be held accountable is critical to the success of your implementation and the increased instructional capacity that will result. Use the twenty-day (student attendance days) Teacher Team Goal-Setting Worksheet in figure 6.7. Grade-level teams use this format to determine their goals based on assessment results and student work samples, decide on improvement strategies, devise a pretest and posttest, agree on a twenty-day instructional period to attain the established goal, and then use what they have learned together to make instructional improvements. They then reconvene to monitor the goal's status at the conclusion of the twenty instructional days. If the goal has been reached, the team engages in another cycle of embedded professional development and goal setting. If their goal is still not met, a meeting with the team and some support staff should be held to determine the kind and amount of support this team needs.

Figure 6.7: Teacher Team Goal-Setting Worksheet

Directions: In thirty minutes or less, engage in this goal-setting process with your team members, and submit it to the principal. Make a copy for each team member.

Brainstorming	
Data used to present evidence of the problem:	
Problem(s) the data suggest:	
Probable causes for this problem:	
Solutions to solve this problem:	
After the Brainstorming	
Best ideas:	
How results will be measured:	
Likelihood of success:	
Clear, measurable, attainable, and compelling goal for what your students will achieve as an outcome of your implementation:	

*Visit **go.solution-tree.com/literacy** to download and print this figure.*

Some teams may share the workload more efficiently if they have the Action Log shown in figure 6.8 (page 120) to hold everyone accountable.

Figure 6.8: Teacher Team Action Log

Activity	By Whom	By When	Resources	Completed
Action Plan Manager:				

*Visit **go.solution-tree.com/literacy** to download and print this figure.*

Phase 6f: Reassess Instructional Capacity

Once all teacher teams have unpacked the selected look-for, designed and delivered a one-minute presentation, developed a twenty-day student achievement goal (twenty student attendance days), implemented the plan, and shared their results with other teams, it's your turn to get back into the act. Engage in another round of classroom walkthroughs (twenty student attendance days) to see how instructional capacity is building across your school as a result of embedded professional development and increased academic focus resulting from grade-level goals. What you hope to see—and what I'm convinced you *will* see—is not only increased instructional capacity as a result of teachers' professional growth, but increased academic capacity shown on both formative and student assessments. Less visible, but nonetheless present, will be increased leadership capacity on the part of teachers who have taken part in productive teacher teams, made presentations to faculty, and served as advisors to you during the process.

The Next Step

You are ready to take the final step! In chapter 7, we will raise expectations for you and your teachers once again, as you engage in classroom walkthroughs together to collect frequency data on the look-fors teachers have unpacked in their collaborative grade-level teams. You and each team will debrief together following each walkthrough.

Chapter 7

Use Team Walkthroughs to Build School Capacity

We have a plethora of seminars in which people [teachers] sit and listen to ideas and concepts. We human beings can learn some things those ways—mostly specific cognitive content. But many things about organizations [schools], operations [curriculum and instruction], and people [students] can only be learned by firsthand experience. The tangible, physical, material aspects of knowledge acquisition and knowledge transfer, learning by doing, learning by coaching and teaching, are critical.

—Pfeffer & Sutton (2000, p. 250)

---

1. Understand the literacy look-fors.

2. Understand the classroom walkthroughs.

3. Assess your instructional leadership capacity.

4. Orient your faculty to the look-fors and walkthroughs.

5. Collect and analyze look-for frequency data.

6. Develop, implement, and assess embedded professional development.

7. **Use team walkthroughs to build school capacity.**

You have now reached the most exciting step in your school's implementation of the literacy look-fors and walkthroughs: using grade-level team walkthroughs to build school capacity. In this chapter, you and your teachers will begin to simultaneously build instructional, academic, and leadership capacities, as you go on two- to three-minute walkthroughs searching for the literacy look-for your teachers unpacked in their grade-level teams.

Immediately following the walkthroughs, you and the team will spend thirty minutes debriefing about what they saw and the implications of their observations for their own classroom instruction.

If you have been reluctant about stepping up to this last step because you have heard rumors of teachers who told colleagues they are going to lock their doors, review the section on assertiveness in chapter 3 (page 60). Classroom walkthroughs with grade-level teams will break down the isolation and lack of trust by giving teachers a common language to talk about instruction and a common purpose—increasing literacy levels. The more isolated, private, and distrustful your teachers are, the more traumatic they will find this process. The key to success is having very specific debriefing guidelines, a collaboratively developed professional code, and a strong commitment to adhere personally to these documents in order to build relational trust with your teachers.

I enjoy reading books written for the corporate world, looking for strategies that will transfer from boardrooms to classrooms. One of my favorites is *The Knowing-Doing Gap: How Smart Companies Turn Knowledge Into Action* (Pfeffer & Sutton, 2000). This knowing-doing gap is epidemic in many schools today. The majority of the professional development opportunities available to teachers involve gaining knowledge—listening to speakers, watching PowerPoints, and taking notes in binders. As a professional developer, I build in multiple opportunities during a daylong workshop for teachers to practice various reading interventions with a partner or take turns teaching a lesson to their tablemates. However, these brief moments do not provide time for participants to observe the teaching of real students in real time and then to reflect about what they observed with grade-level colleagues.

I have been privileged during my career to walk through hundreds of classrooms around the country. In fact, that's how I learned to teach in the beginning—by watching other professionals teach: the supervising teachers from my student teaching days, the classroom teachers with whom I worked as a media specialist for seven years, and the classroom teachers I supervised during my years as a principal and assistant superintendent.

Unfortunately for most teachers, once they have a certificate, they rarely have opportunities to learn from watching others teach or to cognitively process what they have observed with other educators. Regrettably, the majority of elementary teachers around the country have never walked through the classrooms of their school to observe their colleagues teaching.

This final step in the implementation process is packed with power. I have not placed it last because it is the least important, but because it is the most important. Before you were ready to implement classroom walkthroughs with teacher teams, there was groundwork to be laid. The tender seeds you have planted since you began your implementation—that one can assess the instructional capacity of a school through collecting look-for frequency data, that collaborative grade-level teams can be responsible for their own professional growth and held accountable for student growth based on what they learned, and that watching others teach can be an exciting, growth-evoking experience for both the observer and the observed—have hopefully taken root in your school. Now it's time to use the literacy look-fors to guide your classroom walkthroughs with teachers. You will be amazed at the growth of professionalism and the renewed focus on teaching and learning.

The Challenges of Grade-Level Literacy Walkthroughs

Do remember, however, that taking grade-level teams on walkthroughs is a high-risk activity requiring knowledge about literacy, ground rules, guidelines, and practice. Here are some of the challenges you will face as you undertake this final step.

Suspending Judgment

If you are like most principals (myself included) you have developed a habit of walking into a classroom and making a snap judgment about the rightness or wrongness of what you see. Recall the question and answer section from chapter 2 (page 51) in which we addressed this issue. That's why it may have been difficult when you first began collecting data to decide whether you saw a look-for or didn't see it and quickly move on. Conducting the pilot walkthroughs was the beginning step in getting rid of that "judgmental stance."

That same stance colors the feelings of the teachers you observe. They just want to know whether you think what they are doing is okay. They don't necessarily want to reflect about the whys and wherefores with you or anybody else. They want to be assured of a satisfactory evaluation. They may even lower their expectations to satisfy you if your expectations aren't sufficiently high.

This judgmental approach to classroom visitations colors the walkthrough experience from both perspectives. The principal's perspective is rooted in the need to have evidence for the evaluations that must be written. I see this need manifested in the principals who want to fill out individual data sheets on teachers and retain them in their files. Add to these two perspectives the feelings and fears of a grade-level team of teachers engaging in a walkthrough for the first time as well as the host teachers they will observe, and you will be able to cut the tension with a knife. This is a temporary state of affairs. Your first job as administrator during this implementation is to continually remind everyone that the frequency data you collected during classroom walkthroughs will not be used to evaluate individual teachers, and that the observations and conversations that are a part of team walkthroughs and debriefings will be held in strictest confidence. Your second job is to make sure that you keep this promise.

Dealing With New Expectations

All of the steps in the implementation of literacy look-fors to this point have been fairly straightforward and low risk, for both you and your teachers. The first six steps required doing some homework and perhaps putting in additional hours on the job, but you have felt confident of your abilities to handle these challenges. However, dismantling your school's privacy norms that have been there as long as the plaster on the walls may create some consternation among teachers. There may even be some new expectations that you had not anticipated when you began the process.

The Need to Provide Instructional Support for Struggling Teachers

When you open up your school to the entire staff, there will be those less than stellar teachers who will suddenly be teaching in a spotlight. If you have been reluctant to address the instructional weaknesses of these staff members for any number of what can often seem to be logical reasons, including yearly promises of retirement or political realities, now is the time to do so. Do you have a plan?

The Need to Provide Team-Building Support for Grade-Level Teams

Prior to implementing literacy look-fors and walkthroughs, you could easily ignore a dysfunctional grade-level team. Oh, you might have reassigned teachers here and there to balance specific teams, but now, collaborative grade-level teams will be the foundation of your professional development and the primary way to build instructional capacity. If some teams aren't working well together, how will you handle this challenge?

Prepping Teachers for Classroom Walkthroughs

Conducting classroom walkthroughs with grade-level teams and debriefing immediately afterward offers opportunities for shared inquiry, acquiring new knowledge about literacy learning, and professionalizing instruction. Critical to successful debriefings is adherence by all participants to a set of agreed-upon guidelines and a Professional Standards Code.

Prepare a set of debriefing guidelines for each new teacher team. Although each member received copies in his or her orientation packet, this copy will be signed and returned to you. Ask each individual to sign a form. This is not a legal document and there is no requirement that teachers sign it. It is a pro forma pledge of each teacher's willingness to be discreet. There may be some teachers who refuse to sign the form out of their fear of the walkthroughs process. Don't turn this refusal into a showdown. Privately say to any teacher who refuses to sign, "Your refusal to sign is sending a message to your teammates and also to the host teachers in whose classrooms you will be observing that you want to be able to say whatever you want to after you go on a walkthrough, including gossiping or telling untruths. What about the teachers who will walk through *your* classroom? Don't you want them to maintain confidentiality and professionalism after being in *your* classroom?"

Debriefing With a Teacher Team After Classroom Walkthroughs

As you and your staff become more comfortable with the look-fors and walkthroughs, the guidelines and procedures may be relaxed a bit at your discretion. However, for a school in which the privacy norms have been exceptionally strong, everyone's strict adherence to the guidelines is crucial for a smooth start. The principal is responsible for doing the following during the debriefing session:

- ❏ Articulate the guidelines for discussion during the debriefing meeting and for professional responsibilities after the meeting.

- ❏ Model professional contributions about the observations in accordance with the guidelines.

- ❏ Hold team members accountable for professional contributions by calling a brief time out if any team member violates the professional standards.

❏   Hold team members accountable for any inappropriate statements
    made to another team member in violation of the professional
    standards agreement by requesting an apology for the violation and
    politely moving the meeting on.

❏   The use of learning stems is optional, but is recommended during
    the first round of teacher contributions. Figure 7.1 contains a set
    of teacher contributions from a debriefing meeting after a teacher
    team went looking for scaffolding in three different classrooms. The
    italicized portion of the sentence is the learning stem, while the
    remainder of the sentence is what individuals added to communicate
    their observations.

**Figure 7.1: Teacher Comments Using Learning Stems During a
Debriefing Meeting**

Speaker	Comment Using a Learning Stem
Teacher 1	*I am wondering how teachers generally* figure out exactly when to scaffold.
Teacher 2	*I'm impatient to start* doing some of the things we saw in our walkthroughs today.
Teacher 3	*I would definitely like to become more expert in* scaffolding. It's not my strongest move.
Teacher 4	*I am trying to solve the puzzle of* the two levels of scaffolding. We weren't looking for the higher-level type today, but I did spot it in one classroom and would like to know more about how that teacher does it.
Teacher 5	*I am curious about* what evidence you saw of the higher-level type of scaffolding.
Principal	*I would like to become more expert* at identifying this look-for during my walkthroughs. Until I studied the protocol you developed (see figure 7.2), I was thinking in terms of one or two things. I can see that your team did a thorough job of unpacking this look-for. OK, how about another go-round of responses.

*Visit **go.solution-tree.com/literacy** to download and print this figure.*

The team used the observation protocol shown in figure 7.2. They
developed it during their month-long embedded professional development
study of the scaffolding literacy look-for. The protocol contains a menu of
ways that teachers can scaffold student learning. The team used a variety of
resources to unpack scaffolding and construct their scaffolding observation
protocol, such as books (McEwan-Adkins, 2010; Wilhelm, Baker, & Dube,
2001), online articles (Dickson, Simmons, & Kame'enui, 1995), and teacher
brainstorming.

Figure 7.2: Scaffolding Look-Fors and Their Definitions

Scaffolding Look-For	Description
Physical Modeling	The teacher provides physical modeling showing students how to do something.
Thinking Aloud	The teacher thinks aloud to show students how she handles something difficult.
Visual Cues	The teacher provides pictures, objects, or graphic organizers.
Cognitive Processing Time	The teacher provides frequent breaks for cognitive processing so students don't have to sit and listen for long periods.
More Practice Time Provided	The teacher provides additional practice for struggling students.
More Wait Time	The teacher provides more wait time for students to both ask and answer questions and to process the answers other students have given.
Priority Seating	The teacher arranges seating in order to maximize eye contact, frequent monitoring, and coaching.
Preteaching Vocabulary	The teacher preteaches key vocabulary using both pictures cues and student-friendly definitions.
Text Preview Before Reading	The teacher provides a thorough text preview before students begin to read the story, giving information about the plot and alerting students to possible difficulties they might have in one or more spots in the story.
Peer Support	The teacher has numbered the class by ones and twos, assigning semi-permanent partners.
Providing More Accessible Text	The teacher provides text that is more accessible so students can practice comprehension strategies and acquire content knowledge.
Breaking Up Task Into Chunks	The teacher breaks up difficult tasks into more discrete chunks or steps enabling students to do one step at a time.
Using a Routine	The teacher uses predictable routines for learning new skills and strategies.
Using Posters or Charts	The teacher provides accessible posters and charts on the wall and for the desktop.
Using Prompts	The teacher teaches sets of prompts that enable students to follow the steps independently.
Lots of Checks for Understanding	The teacher frequently checks for understanding and adds extra information or clarifies for confused students.
Well-Explained Directions	The teacher gives very clear verbal directions that are supplemented with written directions with picture prompts if applicable.

continued →

Scaffolding Look-For	Description
Use of Advance Organizer	The teacher gives students opportunities to figure out what the lesson is about and activates their prior knowledge about previous lessons or life experiences that may be relevant.
Coaching of Individual Students	The teacher keeps a watchful eye on struggling students and frequently offers coaching as appropriate.
Speaking More Slowly	The teacher speaks more slowly, enunciates more clearly, and adds "pause and punch" (more emphasis to certain important words) during instruction.
Pointing Out Words on the Board or Wall When Saying Them	The teacher runs her hand under vocabulary written on the board, drawing the attention of struggling students to the pronunciation, spelling and meaning of the words.
Practicing Difficult Things in Unison to Support Struggling Students	The teacher provides as many "we do its" (teacher and students rehearsing a skill together) as needed for struggling students to achieve mastery.
Providing Pictures and Words Together	The teacher provides picture cues along with words to teach vocabulary.
Not Overloading Students With Too Many Directions or Steps at Once	The teacher limits the number of steps in a process or steps in a set of directions so that students will not be overloaded and confused.
Oral Reading With Students	The teacher orally reads along with students to scaffold the text.

*Visit **go.solution-tree.com/literacy** to download and print this figure.*

The Next Step

The step you take next, now that you have completed the seven steps, depends on your perception of the needs of your school at this point. Since literacy look-fors and walkthroughs are an ongoing process, I recommend that you repeat the following steps.

❑ Continue to dig more deeply into the literacy look-fors, and become increasingly expert about the literacy look-fors.

❑ Continue to assess your school's capacities as needed. Collect and analyze frequency data every other month. Continue to evaluate your leadership capacities by touching base with school leaders to see what else you could be doing to support their grade-level teams.

❑ Look for various ways to customize professional development using research-based books, videos, and the talents of teacher leaders on your staff.

❑ Focus on the improvement of teaching with the goal of increasing student learning once you have learned the process. Use the literacy look-fors to inform what your teachers are doing.

❑ Don't become distracted by the next new thing. Stick with research-based curricula and instruction.

Conclusion

My granddaughter recently started kindergarten. Since her family lives in another country, my daughter graciously keeps me informed of what's happening at school. I was particularly intrigued by one item on the agenda for the opening day of school. It was titled "Primary Commencement." Since there was no possible way for my husband and me to attend this event, my daughter took notes and pictures so she could relay every detail to me. Each kindergarten student was escorted into the auditorium by an upper-class student as solemn music played over the speakers. The stage was lined with shiny gold gift bags, each one adorned by two helium-filled balloons, one gold and one purple, the school colors. The headmaster explained to the new students and parents the meaning of *commencement*—the beginning of something: their formal education. In a way he was initiating them into the expectations of the school, since the gifts they found in their bags were symbolic of the different things they would be learning: a pen for writing, a book for reading, and a dictionary for acquiring new words. When he had finished with his short speech, he called each kindergarten student by name to come to stage individually. I saw the photo of our granddaughter climbing the steep stairs from the auditorium floor to the stage, walking across it, shaking hands with the headmaster, and then with a big smile claiming her bag. This was a commencement I will never forget, even thought I experienced it vicariously. I hope my granddaughter will not forget it either.

The heading for this section suggests that your work is finished, but in reality it is just beginning. I hope that this conclusion will be a commencement for you and your teachers—the commencement of a commitment to collaboration in grade-level teams focused on what you have collectively learned about research-based reading instruction working with the literacy look-fors. I am certain that you and your staff will discover a huge reservoir of untapped capacity within each student and teacher and administrator if only you will open the classroom doors of your school and walk through them daily with collaborative teacher teams. Raising literacy levels for all students, no matter their demographics, can only be done collectively.

I became a fan of Jim Collins when I wrote *10 Traits of Highly Effective Principals: From Good to Great Performance* (2003). He reminds us that getting to a great performance depends more on consistency and constancy than on flashes of brilliance.

> Good to great comes by a cumulative process—step by step, action by action, decision by decision, turn upon turn of the flywheel—that adds up to sustained and spectacular results . . . . . . By pushing in a constant direction over an extended period of time, they [the leaders of a corporation] inevitably hit a point of breakthrough. (2003, p. 169)

Dennis Sparks (2005) offers these words of warning:

> There is very little that can hold you and your staff back, with three exceptions: (1) a lack of clarity about your beliefs and values, (2) dependence on those outside of the school for solutions to problems, and (3) a sense of resignation that robs educators of the energy that is essential to the continuous improvement of teaching, learning, and relationships in schools. (p. 162)

Finally, I leave you with these words of encouragement. There is one thing that can handle all three of these roadblocks: collaborative grade-level teams committed to working together to do the challenging work of keeping literacy levels high for all students. As these teams continue to pass the torch of literacy teaching to novice teachers and inexperienced administrators and continue to motivate newly enrolled students, there will be opportunities for literacy learning and attainment for every student.

References and Resources

Adams, G., & Carnine, D. (2003). Direct instruction. In H. L. Swanson, K. R. Harris, & S. Graham (Eds.), *Handbook of learning disabilities* (pp. 403–416). New York: Guilford Press.

Adams, M. J. (1990). *Beginning to read*. Cambridge, MA: MIT Press.

Adams, M. J. (1998). The three-cueing system. In J. Osborn & F. Lehr (Eds.), *Literacy for all: Issues in teaching and learning* (pp. 73–99). New York: Guilford Press.

Afflerbach, P. (1990a). The influence of prior knowledge and text genre on readers' prediction strategies. *Reading Research Quarterly, 22*, 131–148.

Afflerbach, P. (1990b). The influence of prior knowledge on expert readers' main idea strategies. *Reading Research Quarterly, 25*, 31–46.

Afflerbach, P. (2002). Teaching reading self-assessment strategies. In C. C. Block & M. Pressley (Eds.), *Comprehension instruction: Research-based best practices* (pp. 96–111). New York: Guilford Press.

Ainsworth, L. (2003). *Power standards: Identifying the standards that matter most*. Englewood, CO: Advanced Learning Press.

Allington, R. L. (1980). Teacher interruption behaviors during primary grade oral reading. *Journal of Educational Psychology, 72*, 371–377.

Allington, R. L. (2001). *What really matters for struggling readers*. New York: Addison-Wesley Longman.

Anderson, L. M., Evertson, C. M., & Emmer, E. T. (1979, April). *Dimensions in classroom management derived from recent research*. Paper presented at the annual meeting of the American Educational Research Association, San Francisco, CA.

Anderson, R. C. (1975). Student involvement in learning and school achievement. *California Journal of Educational Research, 26*, 53–62.

Anderson, R. C., Wilson, P. T., & Fielding, L. G. (1988). Growth in reading and how children spend their time outside of school. *Reading Research Quarterly, 23*(3), 285–303.

Apel, K. (2007, March). *Word study: Using a five-block approach to improving literacy skills.* Paper presented at the Texas School Health Association, Austin, TX.

Apel, K., & Masterson, J. J. (2001). Theory-guided spelling assessment and intervention. *Language, Speech, and Hearing Services in Schools, 32,* 182–195.

Apel, K., Masterson, J. J., & Niessen, N. L. (2004). Spelling assessment frameworks. In A. Stone, E. R. Silliman, & L. C. Wilkinson (Eds.), *Language and literacy learning in schools* (pp. 292–315). New York: Guilford Press.

APQC Education Group. (2009). *Evaluating professional learning communities: An APQC benchmarking project—A final report.* Houston, TX: Author.

Arter, J. A., & Chappuis, J. (2006). *Creating and recognizing quality rubrics.* Boston: Allyn & Bacon.

Aspy, D. N., & Roebuck, F. N. (1977). *Kids don't learn from people they don't like.* Amherst, MA: Human Resource Development Press.

Ayres, I. (2007). *Super crunchers: Why thinking-by-numbers is the new way to be smart.* New York: Bantam Books.

Bakunas, B., & Holley, W. (2004). Teaching organizational skills. *The Clearing House, 77*(3), 92–95.

Ball, E. W., & Blachman, B. A. (1991). Does phoneme awareness training in kindergarten make a difference in early word recognition and developmental spelling? *Reading Research Quarterly, 24*(1), 49–66.

Bardwell, R. (1984). The development and motivation functions of expectations. *American Educational Research Journal, 21,* 461–472.

Barnes, F., Miller, M., & Dennis, R. (2001). Face to face. *Journal of Staff Development, 22*(4), 42–43, 47.

Barth, R. S. (1990). *Improving schools from within: Teachers, parents, and principals can make the difference.* San Francisco: Jossey-Bass.

Beck, I. L., & McKeown, M. G. (1991). Conditions of vocabulary acquisition. In R. Barr, M. L. Kamil, P. B. Mosenthal, & P. D. Pearson (Eds.), *Handbook of reading research* (Vol. 2, pp. 789–814). New York: Longman.

Beck, I. L., McKeown, M. G., & Kucan, L. (2002). *Bringing words to life: Robust vocabulary instruction.* New York: Guilford Press.

Bereiter, C. (2002). *Education and mind in the knowledge age.* Mahwah, NJ: Erlbaum.

Bereiter, C., & Bird, M. (1985). Use of thinking aloud in identification and teaching of reading comprehension strategies. *Cognition and Instruction, 2*(2), 131–156.

Bereiter, C., & Scardamalia, M. (1987). *The psychology of written composition.* Hillsdale, NJ: Erlbaum.

Berninger, V. W., Vaughan, K., Abbott, R. D., Begay, K., Coleman, K., Byrd, K., et al. (2002). Teaching spelling and composition alone and together: Implications for the simple view of writing. *Journal of Educational Psychology, 94*, 291–304.

Blachman, B., Ball, E., Black, R., & Tangel, D. (1994). Kindergarten teachers develop phoneme awareness in low-income, inner-city classrooms: Does it make a difference? *Reading and Writing, 6*, 1–17.

Black, P., Harrison, C., Lee, C., Marshall, B., & Wiliam, D. (2003). *Assessment for learning: Putting it into practice.* New York: Open University Press.

Black, P., & Wiliam, D. (1998). *Inside the black box: Raising standards through classroom assessment.* London: School of Education, King's College.

Blatt, B., Linsley, B., & Smith, L. (2005). Classroom walk-throughs their way. *UCLA SMP EdNews.* Accessed at www.smp.gseis.ucla.edu/Resources/EdNews /ednews_2005_01.html on June 1, 2010.

Block, J. H. (1971). *Mastery learning: Theory and practice.* New York: Holt, Rinehart & Winston.

Block, J. H., & Anderson, L. W. (1975). *Mastery learning in classroom instruction.* New York: Macmillan.

Bloom, B. S. (1971). *Mastery learning.* New York: Holt, Rinehart & Winston.

Bloom, B. S. (1974). Time and learning. *American Psychologist, 29*, 682–688.

Bloom, B. S. (1980). The new direction in educational research: Alterable variables. *Phi Delta Kappan, 61*, 382–385.

Bogner, K., Raphael, L. M., & Pressley, M. (2002). How grade-1 teachers motivate literate activity by their students. *Scientific Studies of Reading, 6*(2), 135–165.

Borich, G. D. (2000). *Effective teaching methods* (4th ed.). Upper Saddle River, NJ: Merrill.

Borkowski, J. G., & Muthukrishna, N. (1992). Moving metacognition into the classroom: "Working models" and effective strategy teaching. In M. Pressley, K. R. Harris, & J. T. Guthrie (Eds.), *Promoting academic competence and literacy in school* (pp. 477–501). San Diego: Academic Press.

Bosman, A. M. T., & Van Ordern, G. C. (1997). Why spelling is more difficult than reading. In C. A. Perfetti, L. Riegen, & M. Fayol (Eds.), *Learning to spell: Research, theory, and practice across languages* (pp. 173–194). Mahwah, NJ: Erlbaum.

Bossidy, L., & Charan, R. (2002). *Execution: The discipline of getting things done.* New York: Crown.

Bransford, J. D. (1984). Schema activation—schema acquisition. In R. C. Anderson, J. Osborn, & R. C. Tierney (Eds.), *Learning to read in American schools* (pp. 258–272). Hillsdale, NJ: Erlbaum.

Bransford, J. D., Brown, A. L., & Cocking R. R. (2000). *How people learn: Brain, mind, experience & school.* Washington, DC: National Academies Press.

Bransford, J. D., Darling-Hammond, L., & LePage, P. (2005). Introduction. In L. Darling-Hammond, J. Bransford, P. LePage, K. Hammerness, & H. Duffy (Eds.), *Preparing teachers for a changing world: What teachers should learn and be able to do* (pp. 1–39). San Francisco: Jossey-Bass.

Brenner, D., Tompkins, R., Hiebert, E., Riley, M., & Miles, R. (2007, May). *Eyes on the page: A large-scale intervention to increase time spent reading accessible texts.* Paper presented at the 2007 International Reading Association Annual Convention, Toronto, Ontario, Canada.

Brophy, J. E. (1981). Teacher praise: A functional analysis. *Review of Educational Research, 51,* 5–32.

Brophy, J. E. (1985). Teachers' expectations, motives and goals for working with problem students. *Research on Motivation in Education: The Classroom Milieu, 2,* 175–214.

Brophy, J. E. (1987). Synthesis of research on strategies for motivating students to learn. *Educational Leadership, 45*(2), 40–48.

Brophy, J. E. (1999). *Teaching.* Brussels, Belgium: International Academy of Education.

Brophy, J. E., & Good, T. L. (1986). Teacher behavior and student achievement. In M. C. Wittrock (Ed.), *Handbook of research on teaching* (3rd ed., pp. 328–375). Upper Saddle River, NJ: Merrill/Prentice Hall.

Brown, A. L., & Campione, J. C. (1994). Guided discovery in a community of learners. In K. McGilly (Ed.), *Classroom lessons: Integrating cognitive theory and classroom practice* (pp. 229–270). Cambridge, MA: MIT Press.

Brown, A. L., Smiley, S. S., Day, J. D., Townsend, M. A. R., & Lawton, S. D. (1977). Intrusion of a thematic idea in children's comprehension and retention of stories. *Child Development, 48,* 1454–1466.

Bryk, A. S., & Schneider, B. (2002). *Trust in schools: A core resource for improvement.* New York: SAGE.

Burns, J. M. (1978). *Leadership.* New York: Harper & Row.

Bursuck, W. D., & Blanks, B. (2010). Evidence-based early reading practices within a response to intervention system. *Psychology in the Schools, 47*(5), 421–431.

Bursuck, W. D., & Damer, M. (2010). *Reading instruction for students who are at risk or have disabilities.* New York: Pearson.

Byrne, B., & Fielding-Barnsley, R. (1989). Phonemic awareness and letter knowledge in the child's acquisition of the alphabetic principle. *Journal of Educational Psychology, 81,* 313–321.

Byrne, B., & Fielding-Barnsley, R. (1993). Evaluation of a program to teach phonemic awareness to young children: A 1-year follow-up. *Journal of Educational Psychology, 85,* 488–503.

Byrne, B., & Fielding-Barnsley, R. (1995). Evaluation of a program to teach phonemic awareness to young children: A 2-and 3-year follow-up and a new preschool trial. *Journal of Educational Psychology, 87,* 488–503.

Cabello, V., & Terrell, R. (1993). Making students feel like family: How teachers create warm and caring classroom climates. *Journal of Classroom Instruction, 29,* 17–23.

Caine, R. N., & Caine, G. (1994). *Making connections: Teaching and the human brain.* Alexandria, VA: Association for Supervision and Curriculum Development.

Carlson, C, & Brosnahan, E. (2009). *Guiding students into information literacy: Strategies for teachers and teacher-librarians.* Lanham, MD: Scarecrow Press.

Carr, E., & Ogle, D. (1987). K-W-L Plus: A strategy for comprehension and summarization. *Journal of Reading, 30*(7), 626–631.

Carroll, J. B. (1989). The Carroll model: A 25-year retrospective and prospective view. *Educational Researcher, 8*(1), 26–31.

Carroll, T., & Doerr, H. (2010, June 28). Learning teams and the future of teaching. *Education Week.* Accessed at www.edweek.org/ew/articles/2010/06/28 /36carroll.h29.html?qs=Learning+teams+and+the+future+of+teaching on October 1, 2010.

Castle, J. M., Riach, J., & Nicholson, T. (1994). Getting off to a better start in reading and spelling: The effects of phonemic awareness instruction within a whole language program. *Journal of Educational Psychology, 86,* 350–359.

Center for Comprehensive School Reform and Improvement. (2007). *Using classroom walk-throughs as an instructional leadership tool.* Accessed at www.centerforsri.org /index.php?option=com_content&task=view&id=424&Itemid=5 on June 15, 2010.

City, E. A., Elmore, R. F., Fiarman, S. E., & Teitel, L. (2009). *Instructional rounds in education: A network approach to improving teaching and learning.* Cambridge, MA: Harvard Education Press.

Collins, A. (1991). Reading instruction that increases thinking abilities. *Journal of Reading, 34,* 510–516.

Collins, A., Brown, J. S., & Holum, A. (1991, Winter). Cognitive apprenticeship: Making thinking visible. *American Educator,* 6–11, 38–41.

Collins, A., Brown, J. S., & Newman, S. E. (1989). Cognitive apprenticeship: Teaching the crafts of reading, writing, and mathematics. In L. Resnick (Ed.), *Knowing, learning, and instruction: Essays in honor of Robert Glaser* (pp. 453–494). Hillsdale, NJ: Erlbaum.

Collins, J. (1998). *Strategies for struggling writers.* New York: Guilford Press.

Collins, J. (2001). *Good to great: Why some companies make the leap . . . and others don't.* New York: Harper Business.

Collins, J., Lee, J., Fox, J., & Madigan, T. (2008). *When writing serves reading: Randomized trials of writing intensive reading comprehension (WIRC) in low-performing urban elementary schools.* Unpublished manuscript, State University of New York, Buffalo.

Collins, J., Madigan, T., & Lee, J. (2008). *Using thinksheets to improve higher-level literacy.* Manuscript submitted for publication.

Connor, C. M., Morrison, F. J., Fishman, B. J., Schatschneider, C., & Underwood, P. (2007). Algorithm-guided individualized reading instruction. *Science, 315*(5811), 464–465.

Connor, C. M., Morrison, F. J., & Katch, L. E. (2004). Beyond the reading wars: Exploring the effect of child-instruction interactions on growth in early reading. *Scientific Studies of Reading, 8*(4), 305–336.

Connor, C. M., Morrison, F. J., & Petrella, J. N. (2004). Effective reading comprehension instruction: Examining child x instruction interactions. *Journal of Educational Psychology, 96*(4), 682–698.

Connor, C. M., Morrison, F. J., & Slominski, L. (2006). Preschool instruction and children's literacy skill growth. *Journal of Educational Psychology, 98*(4), 665–689.

Connor, C. M., Schatschneider, C., Fishman, B., & Morrison, F. J. (2008, June). *Individualizing student literacy instruction: Exploring causal implications of child x instruction interactions.* Paper presented at the Institute of Education Sciences, Washington, DC.

Corcoran, T., & Goertz, M. (1995). Instructional capacity and high performance schools. *Educational Researcher, 24*(9), 27–31.

Covington, M. V. (1984). The self-worth theory of achievement motivation: Findings and implications. *Elementary School Journal, 85*(10), 5–20.

Craik, F. I. M., & Tulving, E. (195). Depth of processing and the retention of words in episodic memory. *Journal of Experimental Psychology: General, 104*, 268–294.

Cunningham, A. E. (1990). Explicit versus implicit instruction in phonemic awareness. *Journal of Experimental Child Psychology, 50*, 429–444.

Davey, B. (1983). Think aloud: Modeling the cognitive processes of reading comprehension. *Journal of Reading, 27*(1), 44–47.

Davey, B., & McBride, S. (1986). Effects of question-generation on reading comprehension. *Journal of Educational Psychology, 78*, 256–262.

Dickinson, D. K., & Tabors, P. O. (2001). *Beginning literacy with language: Young children learning at home and school.* Baltimore: Brookes.

Dickson, S. V., Collins, V. L., Simmons, D. C., & Kame'enui, E. J. (1998). Meta-cognitive strategies: Instructional and curricular basics and implications. In D. C. Simmons & E. J. Kame'enui (Eds.), *What reading research tells us about children with diverse learning needs* (pp. 361–380). Hillsdale, NJ: Erlbaum.

Dickson, S. V., Simmons, D. C., & Kame'enui, E. (1995). *Text organization: Curricular and instructional implications for diverse learners* (Tech. Rep. No. 18). Eugene, OR: National Center to Improve the Tools of Educators. Accessed at www.eric.ed.gov/ERICWebPortal/recordDetail?accno=ED386865 on April 14, 2011. (ERIC Document Reproduction Service No. ED386865)

Dole, J. A. (2000). Explicit and implicit instruction in comprehension. In B. M. Taylor, M. F. Graves, & P. van den Broek (Eds.), *Reading for meaning: Fostering comprehension in the middle grades* (pp. 52–69). New York: Teachers College Press.

Dole, J. A., Valencia, S. W., Greer, E. A., & Wardrop, J. L. (1991). Effects of two types of prereading instruction on the comprehension of narrative and expository text. *Reading Research Quarterly, 26*(2), 142–159.

Dolezal, S. E., Welsh, L. M., Pressley, M., & Vincent, M. M. (2003). How nine third-grade teachers motivate student academic engagement. *The Elementary School Journal, 103*(3), 239–267.

Dorn, L. J., French, C., & Jones, T. (1998). *Apprenticeship in literacy.* Portland, ME: Stenhouse.

Dowhower, S. L. (1987). Effects of repeated reading on second-grade transitional readers' fluency and comprehension. *Reading Research Quarterly, 22,* 389–406.

Downey, C. J., Steffy, B. E., English, F. W., Frase, L. E., & Poston, W. K. (2004). *The three-minute classroom walk-through: Changing school supervisory practice one teacher at a time.* Thousand Oaks, CA: Corwin Press.

Duffy, G. G. (2002). The case for direct explanation of strategies. In C. C. Block & M. Pressley (Eds.), *Comprehension instruction: Research-based best practices* (pp. 28–41). New York: Guilford Press.

Duffy, G. G., Roehler, L. R., & Rackliffe, G. (1986). How teachers' instructional talk influences students' understanding of lesson content. *Elementary School Journal, 87*(1), 3–16.

Duffy, G. G., Roehler, L. R., Sivan, E., Rackliffe, G., Book, C., Meloth, M., et al. (1987). The effects of explaining the reasoning associated with using reading strategies. *Reading Research Quarterly, 22*(3), 347–368.

DuFour, R. (2007, August 30). We're already a "good" school, why do we need to improve? Accessed at www.allthingsplc.info/wordpress/?p=48 on October 10, 2010.

DuFour, R., & Eaker, R. (1998). *Professional learning communities at work™: Best practices for enhancing student achievement.* Bloomington, IN: Solution Tree Press.

DuFour, R., Eaker, R., & DuFour, R. (Eds.). (2005). *On common ground: The power of professional learning communities.* Bloomington, IN: Solution Tree Press.

Dweck, C. S. (1975). The role of expectations and attributions in the alleviation of learned helplessness. *Journal of Personality and Social Psychology, 31*(4), 674–685.

Ehri, L. C. (1980). Grapheme-phoneme knowledge is essential for learning to read words in English. In J. Metsala & L. Ehri (Eds.), *Word recognition in beginning reading* (pp. 3–40). Hillsdale, NJ: Erlbaum.

Ehri, L. C. (1995). Teachers need to know how word reading processes develop to teach reading effectively to beginners. In C. N. Hedley, P. Antonacci, & M. Rabinowitz (Eds.), *Thinking and literacy: The mind at work* (pp. 167–188). Hillsdale, NJ: Erlbaum.

Ehri, L. C. (1997a). Learning to read and learning to spell are one and the same, almost. In C. A. Perfetti, L. Rieben, & M. Fayoln (Eds.), *Learning to spell: Research, theory, and practice across languages* (pp. 237–269). Mahwah, NJ: Erlbaum.

Ehri, L. C. (1997b). Sight word learning in normal readers and dyslexics. In B. A. Blachman (Ed.), *Foundations in reading acquisition and dyslexia: Implications for early interventions* (pp. 163–190). Mahwah, NJ: Erlbaum.

Ehri, L. C. (1998). Grapheme-phoneme knowledge is essential for learning to read words in English. In J. L. Metsala & L. C. Ehri (Eds.), *Word recognition in beginning literacy* (pp. 3–40). Hillsdale, NJ: Erlbaum.

Emmer, E. T., Evertson, C. M., & Anderson, L. (1979). *Effective classroom management at the beginning of the school year.* Austin: Research and Development Center for Teacher Education, University of Texas.

Emmer, E. T., Evertson, C. M., & Anderson, L. (1980). Effective classroom management at the beginning of the school year. *Elementary School Journal, 80*(5), 219–231.

Evertson, C. M. (1989). Improving elementary classroom management: A school-based training program for beginning the year. *Journal of Educational Research, 83*(2), 82–90.

Evertson, C. M., Emmer, E. T., Clements, B., & Worsham, M. E. (1994). *Classroom management for elementary teachers.* Needham Heights, MA: Allyn & Bacon.

Fielding, L. G., & Pearson, P. D. (1994). Reading comprehension: What works. *Educational Leadership, 51*(5), 62–68. Accessed at www.ascd.org/readingroom /edlead/9402/fielding.html on April 12, 2003.

Fisher, C. W. (1978). *Teaching behaviors, academic learning time and student achievement: Final report of phase III-B, beginning teachers' evaluation study* (Tech. Rep. No. V-1). San Francisco: Far West Regional Laboratory.

Fisher, C. W., & Berliner, D. (1985). *Perspectives on instructional time.* Reading, MA: Addison-Wesley Longman.

Fitzgerald, J., & Shanahan, T. (2000). Reading and writing relations and their development. *Educational Psychologist, 35*(1), 39–50.

Florida Center for Reading Research. (2001). *Using student center activities to differentiate reading instruction: A guide for teachers K–5.* Accessed at www.fcrr.org /profdev on February 21, 2011.

Foorman, B. R. (2007). Primary prevention in classroom reading instruction. *Teaching Exceptional Children, 39*(3), 24–30.

Foorman, B. R., Francis, D. J., Fletcher, J. M., Schatschneider, C., & Mehta, P. (1998). The role of instruction in learning to read: Preventing reading failure in at-risk children. *Journal of Educational Psychology, 90,* 37–55.

Foorman, B. R., Schatschneider, C., Eakin, M. N., Fletcher, J. M., Moats, L. C., & Francis, D. J. (2006). The impact of instructional practices in grades 1 and 2 on reading and spelling achievement in high poverty schools. *Contemporary Educational Psychology, 31,* 1–29.

Foorman, B. R., & Torgesen, J. K. (2001). Critical elements of classroom and small-group instruction promote reading success in all children. *Learning Disabilities Research and Practice, 16*(4), 202–211.

Fuchs, D., Fuchs, L. S., Compton, D. L., Bouton, B., Caffrey, E., & Hill, L. (2007). Dynamic assessment as responsiveness to intervention. *Exceptional Children, 39*(5), 58–63.

Fullan, M. (1998). Leadership for the 21st century: Breaking the bonds of dependency. *Educational Leadership, 55*(7), 6–12.

Fullan, M. (2003). *The moral imperative of the principalship.* Thousand Oaks, CA: Corwin Press.

Gagne, R. M., & Briggs, L. J. (1974). *Principles of instructional design.* New York: Holt, Rinehart and Winston.

Gambrell, L. B. (1996). Creating classroom cultures that foster reading motivation. *Reading Teacher, 50*(1), 14–24.

Gaskins, I. W. (1980). *The benchmark story: The first ten years, 1970–1980.* Media, PA: Benchmark Press.

Gaskins, I. W. (1994). Classroom applications of cognitive science: Teaching poor readers how to learn, think, and problem solve. In K. McGilly (Ed.), *Classroom lessons* (pp. 129–154). Cambridge, MA: MIT Press.

Gaskins, I. W. (2005). *Success with struggling readers: The Benchmark School.* New York: Guilford Press.

Gawande, A. (2009). *The checklist manifesto: How to get things right.* New York: Metropolitan Books.

Gentile, J. R., & Lalley, J. P. (2003). *Standards and mastery learning: Aligning teaching and assessment so all children can learn.* Thousand Oaks, CA: Corwin Press.

Gentile, J. R., Monaco, N. M., Iheozor-Ejiofor, I. E., Ndu, A. N., & Ogbonaya, P. K. (1982). Retention by "fast" and "slow" learners. *Intelligence, 6,* 125–138.

Gentile, J. R., Voelkl, K. E., Mt. Pleasant, J., & Monaco, N. M. (1995). Recall after relearning by fast and slow learners. *Journal of Experimental Education, 63,* 185–197.

Glasser, W. (1969). *Schools without failure.* New York: Harper & Row.

Glasser, W. (1997). *The quality school: Managing schools without coercion.* New York: Harper.

Good, T., & Grouws, D. (1979). The Missouri teacher effectiveness program. *Journal of Educational Psychology, 71,* 355–362.

Goodrich, H. (1997). Understanding rubrics. *Educational Leadership, 54*(4), 14–17.

Gower, R. R., & Scott, M. B. (1977). *Five essential dimensions of curriculum design.* Dubuque, IA: Kendall Hunt.

Graham, S., & Perin, D. (2007). *Writing next: Effective strategies to improve writing of adolescents in middle and high schools.* New York: Alliance for Education.

Graves, M. F., Juel, C., & Graves, B. B. (2004). *Teaching reading in the 21st century* (3rd ed.). Boston: Allyn & Bacon.

Greeno, J. B., Collins, A. M., & Resnick, L. B. (1996). Cognition and learning. In D. Berliner & R. Calfee (Eds.), *Handbook of educational psychology* (pp. 63–84). New York: Macmillan.

Gunther, P. L., Reffel, J. M., Barnett, C. A., Lee, J. M., & Patrick, J. (2004). Academic response rates in elementary-school classrooms. *Education and Treatment of Children, 27*(2), 105.

Hall, T. (2009). *Explicit instruction.* Washington, DC: U.S. Department of Education, Office of Special Education Programs.

Hanushek, E. A. (2002). Teacher quality. In L. T. Izumi & W. M. Evers (Eds.), *Teacher quality* (pp. 1–12). Palo Alto, CA: Hoover.

Harris, T. L., & Hodges, R. E. (Eds.). (1995). *The literacy dictionary: The vocabulary of reading and writing.* Newark, DE: International Reading Association.

Hatch, T. (2009, December 9). Four flawed assumptions of school reform. *Education Week, 24,* 32.

Haycock, K. (1998). *Good teaching matters: How well-qualified teachers can close the gap.* Washington, DC: Education Trust.

Haydon, T., Mancil, G. R., & Van Loan, C. (2009). Using opportunities to respond in a general education classroom: A case study. *Education and Treatment of Children, 32*(2), 267–278.

Herber, H. L., & Herber, J. N. (1993). *Teaching in the content areas with reading, writing, and reasoning.* Old Tappan, NJ: Allyn & Bacon.

Heward, W. L. (1994). Three "low-tech" strategies for increasing the frequency of active student response during group instruction. In R. Gardner III, D. M. Sainato, I. O. Cooper, & T. E. Heron (Eds.), *Behavior analysis in education: Focus on measurably superior instruction* (pp. 283–320). Monterey, CA: Brooks/Cole.

Heward, W. L., Gardner, R., III, Cavanaugh, R. A., Courson, F. H., Grossi, T. A., & Barbetta, P. M. (1996). Everyone participates in this class: Using response cards to increase active student response. *Teaching Exceptional Children, 28,* 4–11.

Hiebert, E. H. (2008a). The (mis)match between texts and students who depend on schools to become literate. In E. H. Hiebert & M. Sailors (Eds.), *Finding the right texts: What works for beginning and struggling readers* (pp. 1–22). New York: Guilford.

Hiebert, E. H. (2008b, August). *Strategic vocabulary selection: Choosing words from narrative and informational texts.* Paper presented at the annual conference of the International Reading Association, Atlanta, GA. Accessed at www.textproject.org on November 12, 2008.

Hiebert, E. H., & Fisher, C. W. (2005). A review of the National Reading Panel's studies on fluency: On the role of text. *Elementary School Journal, 105,* 443–360.

Hiebert, E. H., & Fisher, C. W. (2006). Fluency from the first: What works with first graders. In T. Rasinski, C. L. Z. Blachowicz, & K. Lems (Eds.), *Fluency instruction: Research-based best practices* (pp. 279–294). New York: Guilford Press.

Hillson, M., Jones, J. C., Moore, J. W., & Van Devender, F. (1964). A controlled experiment evaluating the effects of a non-graded organization on pupil achievement. *Journal of Educational Research, 57,* 548–550.

Hipp, K., & Huffman, J. (2002, April). *Documenting and examining practices in creating learning communities: Exemplars and non-exemplars.* Paper presented at the annual meeting of the American Educational Research Association, New Orleans, LA.

Hirsch, E. D., Jr. (2003). Reading comprehension requires knowledge—of words and the world. *American Educator, 27*(2), 11–19, 44–45.

Hirsh, S. (2010, February 17). Teacher learning: Sine qua non of school innovation. *Education Week.* Accessed at www.edweek.org/ew/articles/2010/02/17/22hirsh.h29.html?qs=Teacher+learning:+sine+qua+non+of+school+innovation on October 1, 2010.

Hogan, K., & Pressley, M. (Eds.). (1997). *Scaffolding student learning.* Cambridge, MA: Brookline Books.

Hord, S. M. (1997). *Professional learning communities: Communities of continuous inquiry and improvement.* Austin, TX: Southwest Educational Laboratory.

Howard, J. (1990). *The social construction of intelligence.* Lexington, MA: Efficacy Institute.

Howard, J. (1995). You can't get there from here: The need for a new logic in education reform. *Dædalus, 124*(4), 85–92.

Howard, J., & Hammond, R. (1985, September 9). Rumors of inferiority: The hidden obstacles to black success. *The New Republic,* 17–21.

Hunter, M. (1982). *Mastery teaching: Increasing instructional effectiveness in elementary, secondary schools, colleges and universities.* Thousand Oaks, CA: Corwin Press.

Hyerle, D. (1996). *Visual tools for constructing knowledge.* Alexandria, VA: Association for Supervision and Curriculum Development.

Hyerle, D. (Ed.). (2004). *Student successes with thinking maps.* Thousand Oaks, CA: Corwin Press.

Johnson, D. D., Johnson, B. V. H., & Schlicting, K. (2004). Logology: Word and language play. In J. F. Baumann & E. J. Kame'enui (Eds.), *Vocabulary instruction: Research to practice* (pp. 179–200). New York: Guilford Press.

Jones, J. C., Moore, J. W., & Van Devender, F. (1967). A comparison of pupil achievement after one and one-half and three years in a non-graded program. *Journal of Educational Research, 61,* 75–77.

Jordan, H., Mendro, R., & Weerasinghe, D. (1997). *Teacher effects on longitudinal student achievement.* Dallas, TX: Dallas Independent School District.

Joseph, L. M., & Konrad, M. (2009). Have students self-manage their academic performance. *Intervention in School and Clinic, 44*(4), 246–249.

Joyce, B., & Weil, M. (2008). *Models of teaching* (8th ed.). Boston: Allyn & Bacon.

Just, M. A., & Carpenter, P. A. (1987). *The psychology of reading and language comprehension.* Boston: Allyn & Bacon.

Ishikawa, I. (1985). *What is total quality control?* New York: Prentice Hall.

Kelman, M. E., & Apel, K. (2004). Effects of a multiple linguistic and prescriptive approach to spelling instruction: A case study. *Communication Disorders Quarterly, 25*(2), 56–66.

Kern, L., & Clemens, N. H. (2007). Antecedent strategies to promote appropriate classroom behavior. *Psychology in the Schools, 44,* 65–75.

King, A. (1989). Effects of self-questioning training on college students' comprehension of lectures. *Contemporary Educational Psychology, 14,* 366–381.

King, A. (1990). Improving lecture comprehension: Effects of a metacognitive strategy. *Applied Educational Psychology*, *29*, 331–346.

King, A. (1992) Comparison of self-questioning, summarizing, and note taking-review as strategies for learning from lectures. *American Educational Research Journal*, *29*, 303–325.

King, J. R., Biggs, S., & Lipsky, S. (1984). Students' self-questioning and summarizing as reading study strategies. *Journal of Reading Behavior*, *16*(3), 205–218.

Knapp, M. D. (1995). *Teaching for meaning in high-poverty classrooms.* New York: Teachers College Press.

Knapp, M. S., Copland, M. E., & Talbert, J. (2003). *Leading for learning.* Seattle, WA: Center for the Study of Teaching and Policy.

Kounin, J. S. (1977). *Discipline and group management in classrooms* (2nd ed.). Huntington, NY: Krieger.

Kuhn, M. R., & Stahl, S. A. (2003). Fluency: a review of developmental and remedial practices. *Journal of Educational Psychology*, *95*, 3–21.

Kuhn, T. (1996). *The structure of scientific revolutions.* Chicago: University of Chicago Press. (Original work published 1962)

Lalley, J. P., & Gentile, J. R. (2009). Adapting instruction to individuals based on the evidence, what should it mean? *International Journal of Teaching and Learning in Higher Education*, *20*(3), 462–475.

Lambert, N. M., & McCombs, B. L. (1998). Introduction: Learner-centered schools and classrooms as a direction for school reform. In N. Lambert & B. McCombs (Eds.), *How students learn: Reforming school through learner-centered education* (pp. 1–22). Washington, DC: American Psychological Association.

Learning Keys. (2010). *Data walks.* Houston, TX: The Flippen Group. Accessed at www.learningkeys.org/KeyPlays/DataWalks/tabid/103/Default.aspx on June 1, 2010.

Lewin, K. (1947). *Human relations.* Thousand Oaks, CA: SAGE.

Lie, A. (1991). Effects of a training program for stimulating skills in word analysis for first-grade children. *Reading Research Quarterly*, *26*(3), 263–284.

Lundberg, I., Frost, J., & Peterson, O. (1988). Effects of an extensive program for stimulating phonological awareness in pre-school children. *Reading Research Quarterly*, *23*, 263–284.

Marzano, R. (2009a). *Designing and teaching learning goals and objectives.* Englewood, CO: Marzano Research Laboratory.

Marzano, R. (2009b). Setting the record straight on "high-yield" strategies. *Kappan*, *91*(1), 30–37.

Marzano, R. (2009c). *Teaching basic and advanced vocabulary: A framework for direct instruction.* Alexandria, VA: Association for Supervision and Curriculum Development.

Marzano, R., Marzano, J. S., & Pickering, D. J. (2003). *Classroom management that works: Research-based strategies for every teacher.* Alexandria, VA: Association for Supervision and Curriculum Development.

Mason, J., Roehler, L. R., & Duffy, G. G. (1984). A practitioner's model of comprehension instruction. In G. G. Duffy, L. R. Roehler, & J. Mason (Eds.), *Comprehension instruction: Perspectives and suggestions* (pp. 299–314). New York: Longman.

McCormack, R. L., Paratore, J. R., & Dahlene, K. F. (2004). Establishing instruction congruence across learning settings: One path to success for struggling third grade readers. In R. L. McCormack & J. R. Paratore (Eds.), *After early intervention, then what teaching struggling readers in grades 3 and beyond* (pp. 117–136). Newark, DE: International Reading Association.

McCutchen, D., Abbott, R. D., Green, L. R., Beretvas, S. N., Cos, S., Potter, N. S., et al. (2002). Beginning literacy: links among teacher knowledge, teacher practice, and students learning. *Journal of Learning Disabilities, 35,* 69–86.

McEwan, E. K. (1997). *Leading your team to excellence: How to make quality decisions.* Thousand Oaks, CA: Corwin Press.

McEwan, E. K. (2002a). *7 steps to effective instructional leadership.* (2nd ed.). Thousand Oaks, CA: Corwin Press.

McEwan, E. K. (2002b). *Teach them all to read: Catching kids that fall through the cracks.* Thousand Oaks, CA: Corwin Press.

McEwan, E. K. (2003). *10 traits of highly effective principals: From good to great performance.* Thousand Oaks, CA: Corwin Press.

McEwan, E. K. (2004). *7 strategies of highly effective readers: Using cognitive science to boost K–8 achievement.* Thousand Oaks, CA: Corwin Press.

McEwan, E. K. (2005). *How to deal with teachers who are angry, troubled, exhausted, or just plain confused.* Thousand Oaks, CA: Corwin Press.

McEwan, E. K. (2006). *How to survive and thrive in the first three weeks of school.* Thousand Oaks, CA: Corwin Press.

McEwan, E. K. (2009a). *10 traits of highly effective schools: Raising the achievement bar for all students.* Thousand Oaks, CA: Corwin Press.

McEwan, E. K. (2009b) *Teach them all to read: Catching kids before they fall through the cracks* (2nd ed.). Thousand Oaks, CA: Corwin Press.

McEwan-Adkins, E. K. (2010). *40 reading intervention strategies for K–6 students: Research-based support for RTI.* Bloomington, IN: Solution Tree Press.

McEwan-Adkins, E. K. (in press). *Collaborative teacher literacy teams: Connecting professional growth to student achievement.* Bloomington, IN: Solution Tree Press.

McGill-Franzen, A. M., & McDermott, P. (1978, December). *Negotiating a reading diagnosis.* Paper presented at the National Reading Conference, St. Petersburg, FL.

McKean, E. (Ed.). (2005). *New Oxford American dictionary* (2nd ed). New York: Oxford University Press.

Meichenbaum, D., & Biemiller, A. (1998). *Nurturing independent learners: Helping students take charge of their learning.* Cambridge, MA: Brookline Books.

Merrill, M. D., Tennyson, R. D., & Posey, L. O. (1992). *Teaching concepts: an instructional design guide.* Englewood Cliffs, NJ: Educational Technology.

Mertler, C. A. (2003). *Classroom assessment.* Los Angeles: Pyrczak.

Merton, R. (1968). The Matthew effect in science. *Science, 160,* 56–63.

Metropolitan Life Insurance Company. (2009). *The MetLife survey of the American teacher: Collaborating for student success.* New York: Author.

Miller, G. A. (1956). The magical number seven, plus or minus two: Some limits on our capacity for processing information. *Psychological Review, 104,* 3–65.

Mizell, H. (2010, September 22). The misuse of professional development. *Education Week,* 22–23.

Morgan, E. F., Jr., & Stucker, G. R. (1960). The Joplin plan of reading vs. a traditional method. *Journal of Educational Psychology, 51,* 69–73.

Mosteller, F., Light, R., & Sachs, J. (1996). Sustained inquiry in education: Lessons from skill grouping and class size. *Harvard Educational Review, 66*(4), 797–828.

National Center for Educational Accountability. (2005). *California high school best practices study* (Southwest High School, Central Union High School District). Austin, TX: Author.

National Institute of Child Health and Human Development. (2000). *Report of the National Reading Panel: Teaching children to read: An evidence-based assessment of the scientific research literature on reading and its implications for reading instruction: Report of the subgroups* (NIH Publication No. 00-4769). Washington, DC: U.S. Government Printing Office.

National Reading Panel. (2000). *Teaching children to read: An evidence-based assessment of the scientific research literature on reading and its implications for reading instruction: Reports of the subgroups.* Washington, DC: National Institutes of Health, National Institute of Child Health and Human Development.

Neuman, S. B. (1988). Enhancing children's comprehension through previewing. *National Reading Conference Yearbook, 37,* 219–224.

Newmann, F. M., & Wehlage, G. G. (1995). *Successful school restructuring: A report to the public and educators.* Madison: University of Wisconsin Education Center.

Noddings, N. (1984). *Caring.* Berkeley: University of California Press.

Nolte, R. Y., & Singer, H. (1985). Active comprehension: Teaching a process of reading comprehension and its effects on reading achievement. *Reading Teacher, 39,* 24–31.

O'Connor, K. B. (2009). *How to grade for learning.* Thousand Oaks, CA: Corwin Press.

O'Connor, R. E., Jenkins, J. R., & Slocum, T. A. (1993). *Unpacking phonological awareness: Two treatments for low-skilled kindergarten children.* Unpublished manuscript.

O'Connor, R. E., Swanson, H. L., & Geraghty, C. (2010). Improvement in reading rate under independent and difficult text levels: Influences on word and comprehension skills. *Journal of Educational Psychology, 102*(1), 1–19.

Palincsar, A., & Brown, A. L. (1984). Reciprocal teaching of comprehension fostering and monitoring activities. *Cognition and Instruction, 1*(2), 117–175.

Patterson, K. E., & Coltheart, V. (1987). Phonological processes in reading: A tutorial review. In M. Coltheart (Ed.), *Attention and performance: Vol. 12. The psychology of reading* (pp. 421–447). Hillsdale, NJ: Erlbaum.

Pearson, P. D. (2006, March 26). *Reading, rehashing, 'rithmetic* [Letter to the editor]. *New York Times.* Accessed at www.nytimes.com/2006/03/28/opinion/l28educ .html on February 17, 2011.

Pearson, P. D., Cervetti, G., Bravo, M., Hiebert, E. H., & Arya, D. J. (2005, August). *Reading and writing at the service of acquiring scientific knowledge and dispositions: From synergy to identity.* Paper presented at the Edmonton Regional Learning Consortium, Edmonton, AR.

Pearson, P. D., & Fielding, L. (1991). Comprehension instruction. In R. Barr, M. L. Kamil, P. Mosenthal, & P. D. Pearson (Eds.), *Handbook of reading research* (Vol. 2, pp. 815–860). New York: Longman.

Pearson, P. D., & Gallagher, M. C. (1983). The instruction of reading comprehension. *Contemporary Educational Psychology, 8,* 317–344.

Pearson, P. D., Roehler, L. R., Dole, J. A., & Duffy, G. G. (1992). Developing expertise in reading comprehension. In J. Samuels & A. Farstup (Eds.), *What research has to say about reading instruction* (pp. 145–199). Newark, DE: International Reading Association.

Pfeffer, J., & Sutton, R. I. (2000). *The knowing-doing gap: How smart companies turn knowledge into action.* Cambridge, MA: Harvard Business School Press.

Phi Delta Kappa. (1980). *Why do some urban schools succeed? The Phi Delta Kappa study of exceptional elementary schools.* Bloomington, IN: Author.

Pikulski, J. J., & Chard, D. J. (2005). Fluency: Bridge between decoding and comprehension. *Reading Teacher, 58*(6), 510–519.

Pintrich, P., & Schunk, D. (1996). *Motivation in education: Theory, research and applications.* Englewood Cliffs, NJ: Prentice Hall.

Pitler, H., & Goodwin, B. (2008). Classroom walkthroughs: Learning to see the trees *and* the forest. *Changing Schools, 58*, 9–11.

Porter, A. C., & Brophy, J. (1988). Synthesis of research on good teaching: Insights from the work of the Institute for Research on Teaching. *Educational Leadership, 45*(8), 74–85.

Pressley, M. (1998). *Reading instruction that works: The case for balanced teaching.* New York: Guilford Press.

Pressley, M. (2000). Comprehension instruction in elementary school: A quarter-century of reading progress. In B. M. Taylor, M. F. Graves, & P. van den Broek (Eds.), *Reading for meaning: Fostering comprehension in the middle grades* (pp. 32–51). New York: Teachers College Press.

Pressley, M., El-Dinary, P. B., & Brown, R. (1992). Skilled and not-so-skilled reading: Good information processing and not-so-good information processing. In M. Pressley, K. R. Harris, & J. T. Guthrie (Eds.), *Promoting academic competence and literacy in school* (pp. 91–127). San Diego: Academic Press.

Pressley, M., El-Dinary, P. B., Gaskins, I., Schuder, T., Bergman, J. L., & Almasi, R. B. (1992). Beyond direct explanation: Transactional instruction of reading comprehension strategies. *Elementary School Journal, 92*(5), 513–555.

Pressley, M., Raphael, L., Gallagher, J. D., & DiBella, J. (2004). Providence-St. Mel School: How a school that works for African American students works. *Journal of Educational Psychology, 2*(96), 216–235.

Pressley, M., Wharton-McDonald, R., Allington, R., Block, C. C., Morrow, L., & Tracey, D. (2001). A study of effective first grade literacy instruction. *Scientific Studies of Reading, 15*(1), 35–58.

Pressley, M., Wharton-McDonald, R., & Mistretta, J. (1998). Effective beginning literacy instruction: Dialectical, scaffolded, and contextualized. In J. L. Metsala & L. C. Ehri (Eds.), *Word recognition in beginning literacy* (pp. 357–373). Mahwah, NJ: Erlbaum.

Pressley, M., Wharton-McDonald, R., Raphael, L. M., Bogner, K., & Roehrig, A. D. (2001). Exemplary first grade teaching. In B. M. Taylor & P. D. Pearson (Eds.), *Teaching reading: Effective schools and accomplished teachers* (pp. 73–88). Mahwah, NJ: Erlbaum.

Pressley, M., Woloshyn, V., Burkell, J., Carliglia-Bull, T., Lysynchuk, L., McGoldrick, J., et al. (1995). *Cognitive strategy instruction that really improves children's academic performance.* Cambridge, MA: Brookline.

Proly, J. L., Rivers, J., & Schwartz, J. (2009). Text comprehension: Graphic organizers to the rescue. *Perspectives on School-Based Issues, 10,* 82–89.

Punnett, B. (1986). Goal setting and performance among elementary school students. *Journal of Educational Research, 80,* 40–42.

Rack, J. P., Hulme, C., Snowling, J. J., & Wightman, J. (1994). The role of phonology in young children's learning of sight words: The direct-mapping hypothesis. *Journal of Experimental Psychology, 57,* 42–71.

Randolph, J. J. (2007). Meta-analysis of the research on response cards: Effects on test achievement, quick achievement, participation, and off-task behavior. *Journal of Positive Behavior Interventions, 9*(2), 113–128.

Rasinski, T. V. (1990). Effects of repeated reading and listening-while-reading on reading fluency. *Journal of Educational Research, 83,* 147–150.

Rayner, K., & Pollatsek, A. (1989). *The psychology of reading.* Englewood Cliffs, NJ: Prentice Hall.

Reeves, D. B. (2010). *Elements of grading: A guide to effective practice.* Bloomington, IN: Solution Tree Press.

Reitsma, P. (1983). Printed word learning in beginning readers. *Journal of Experimental Child Psychology, 75,* 321–339.

Resnick, L. B. (1995). From aptitude to effort: A new foundation for our schools. *Dædlus, 124 (4),* 55–62.

Resnick, L. B. (1999, June 16). Making America smarter. *Education Week,* 38–40.

Rivkin, E. A., Hanushek, E. A., & Kain, J. F. (2001). *Teachers, schools, and academic achievement.* Washington, DC: National Bureau of Economic Research.

Roberts, T. A. (1988) Development of pre-instruction versus previous experience: Effects on factual and inferential comprehension. *Reading Psychology, 9*(2), 141–157.

Roberts, T. A., & Meiring, A. (2006). Teaching phonics in the context of children's literature or spelling: Influences on first-grade reading, spelling, and writing and fifth-grade comprehension. *Journal of Educational Psychology, 98*(4), 690–713.

Rogoff, B. (1990). *Apprenticeship in thinking: Cognitive development in social context.* New York: Oxford University Press.

Rosenshine, B. (1971). *Teaching behaviors and student achievement.* London: National Foundation for Education Research in England and Wales.

Rosenshine, B. (1979). Content, time, and direct instruction. In P. Peterson & H. Walberg (Eds.), *Research on teaching: Concepts, findings, and implications* (pp. 28–56). Berkeley, CA: McCutchan.

Rosenshine, B. (1981). How time is spent in elementary classrooms. *Journal of Classroom Interaction, 17*(1), 16–25.

Rosenshine, B. (1986). Synthesis of research on explicit teaching. *Educational Leadership, 43*(7), 60–69.

Rosenshine, B. (1997). Advances in research on instruction. In E. J. Kame'enui & D. Chard (Eds.), *Issues in educating students with disabilities* (pp. 197–221). Mahwah, NJ: Erlbaum.

Rosenshine, B., & Berliner, D. C. (1978). Academic engaged time. *British Journal of Teacher Education, 4*, 3–16.

Rosenshine, B., Meister, C., & Chapman, S. (1996). Teaching students to generate questions: A review of the intervention studies. *Review of Educational Research, 66*(2), 181–221.

Samuels, S. J. (1979). The method of repeated readings. *The Reading Teacher, 32*, 403–408.

Santoro, L. E., Coyne, M. D., & Simmons, D. C. (2006). The reading-spelling connection: Developing and evaluating a beginning spelling intervention for children at risk of reading disability. *Learning Disabilities Research & Practice, 21*(2), 122–133.

Saphier, J., & Gower, R. (1997). *The skillful teacher: Building your teaching skills.* Acton, MA: Research for Better Teaching.

Sather, S. E. (2004). *The Spokane school district: Intentionally building capacity that leads to increased student achievement.* Portland, OR: Northwest Regional Educational Laboratory. Accessed at www.nwrel.org/scpd/reengineering/SpokaneSD/index.asp on June 1, 2010.

Saunders, W. M., Goldenberg, C. N., & Gallimore, R. (2009). Increasing achievement by focusing grade-level teams on improving classroom learning: A prospective, quasi-experimental student of Title I schools. *American Educational Research Journal, 46*(4), 1006–1033.

Schmitt, N., & Schmitt, D. (1995). Vocabulary notebooks: theoretical underpinnings and practical suggestions. *ELT Journal, 49*(2), 133–143.

Schmoker, M. (1999). *Results: The key to continuous school improvement* (2nd ed.). Alexandria, VA: Association for Supervision and Curriculum Development.

Schmoker, M. (2010). When pedagogic fads trump priorities. *Education Week, 30*(5), 22–23.

Schunk, D. (1984). Enhancing self-efficacy and achievement through rewards and goals: Motivational and informational effects. *Journal of Educational Research, 78*, 29–34.

Senge, P. (1990). *The fifth discipline: The art and practice of the learning organization.* New York: Doubleday Currency.

Share, D. L. (1999). Phonological recoding and orthographic learning: A direct test of the self-teaching hypothesis. *Journal of Experimental Child Psychology, 72,* 95–129.

Shulman, L. S. (1999). Foreword. In L. Darling-Hammond & G. Sykes (Eds.), *Teaching as the learning profession: Handbook of policy and practice* (pp. xi–xiv). San Francisco: Jossey-Bass.

Silverman, S. L., & Casazza, M. E. (2000). *Learning and development: Making connections to enhance teaching.* San Francisco: Jossey-Bass.

Sinatra, G. M., Stahl-Gemake, J., & Berg, D. N. (1984). Improving reading comprehension of disabled readers through semantic mapping. *Reading Teacher, 38*(1), 22–29.

Singer, H., & Dolan, D. (1982). Active comprehension: Problem-solving schema with question generation of complex short stories. *Reading Research Quarterly, 17,* 166–186.

Smolkin, L. B., & Donovan, C. A. (2000). *The contexts of comprehension: Information book read alouds and comprehension acquisition.* Ann Arbor: University of Michigan School of Education, Center for the Improvement of Early Reading Achievement.

Snow, C. E. (2002). *Reading for understanding: Toward a research and development program in reading comprehension.* Santa Monica, CA: RAND.

Sparks, D. (2005). Leading for transformation. In R. DuFour, R. Eaker, & R. DuFour (Eds.), *On common ground: The power of professional learning communities* (pp. 155–175). Bloomington, IN: Solution Tree Press.

Spiegel, D. L. (1998). Silver bullets, babies, and bath water: Literature response groups in a balanced literacy program. *Reading Teacher, 52*(5), 114–124.

Stahl, R. J. (1994). *Using "think-time" and "wait-time" skillfully in the classroom.* (ERIC Document Reproduction Service No. ED370885)

Stahl, S. A. (1997). *Fluency-oriented reading instruction* (Reading Research Report No. 79). Ann Arbor: University of Michigan Schools of Education, Center for the Improvement of Early Reading Achievement.

Stahl, S. A. (1999). *Vocabulary development.* Cambridge, MA: Brookline.

Stahl, S. A. (2005). Four problems with teaching word meanings and what to do to make vocabulary an integral part of instruction. In E. H. Hiebert & M. L. Kamil (Eds.), *Teaching and learning vocabulary* (pp. 95–114). Mahwah, NJ: Erlbaum.

Stahl, S. A., & Heubach, K. M. (2005). Fluency-oriented reading instruction. *Journal of Literacy Research, 37,* 25–60.

Stallings, J. A. (1980). Allocated academic learning time revisited, or beyond time on task. *Educational Researcher, 9*(11), 11–16.

Stanovich, K. E. (1986). Matthew effects in reading: Some consequences of individual differences in the acquisition of literacy. *Reading Research Quarterly, 21,* 360–407.

Stichter, J. P., Stormont, M., & Lewis, T. J. (2009). Instructional practices and behavior during reading: A descriptive summary and comparison of practices in Title One and non-Title elementary schools. *Psychology in the Schools, 46*(2), 172–183.

Stigler, J. W., & Hiebert, J. (1999). *The teaching gap: Best ideas from the world's teachers for improving education in the classroom.* New York: Free Press.

Stipek, D. J. (1993). *Motivation to learn: From theory to practice.* Needham Heights, MA: Allyn & Bacon.

Stockard, J., & Engelmann, K. (2010). The development of early academic success: The impact of direct instruction's reading mastery. *Journal of Behavior Assessment and Intervention in Children, 1*(1), 2–24.

Tague, N. R. (2004). *The quality toolbox* (2nd ed.). Milwaukee, WI: ASQ Quality Press.

Taylor, B. M., Pearson, P. D., Clark, K., & Walpole, S. (2000). Effective schools and accomplished teachers: Lessons about primary-grade reading instruction in low-income schools. *Elementary School Journal, 101*(2), 121–165.

Tharp, R. G. (1982). The effective instruction of comprehension: Results and description of the Kamehameha Early Education Program. *Reading Research Quarterly, 17*(4), 503–527.

Thompson, C. L., & Zeuli, J. S. (1999). The frame and the tapestry: Standards-based reform and professional development. In L. Darling-Hammond & G. Sykes (Eds.), *Teaching as the learning profession: Handbook of policy and practice* (pp. 341–375). San Francisco: Jossey-Bass.

Timperley, H. S., & Wiseman, J. (2003). *The sustainability of professional development in literacy: Part 2. School-based factors associated with high student achievement.* Wellington, New Zealand: Ministry of Education. Accessed at www.minedu.govt .nz/index.dfm?layout=document&documentid=8638&data=1 on October 7, 2010.

Torgesen, J. K. (2006). *Intensive reading interventions for struggling readers in early elementary school: A principal's guide.* Portsmouth, NH: RMC Research Corporation, Center on Instruction.

Torgesen, J. K., & Hudson, R. F. (2006). Reading fluency: Critical issues for struggling readers. In S. J. Samuels & A. E. Farstrup (Eds.), *What research has to say about fluency instruction* (pp. 130–158). Newark, DE: International Reading Association.

Torgesen, J. K., Wagner, R. K., & Rashotte, C. A. (1997). The prevention and remediation of severe reading disabilities: Keeping the end in mind. *Scientific Studies of Reading, 1,* 217–234.

Trabasso, T., & Bouchard, E. (2000). Text comprehension instruction. *Report of the National Reading Panel: Report of the subgroups* (chap. 4, Pt. 2, pp. 39–69). Washington, DC: NICHD Clearinghouse.

Trabasso, T., & Bouchard, E. (2002). Teaching readers how to comprehend text strategically. In C. C. Block & M. Pressley (Eds.), *Comprehension instruction: Research-based best practices* (pp. 176–200). New York: Guilford Press.

Treiman, R. (1998). Why spelling? The benefits of incorporating spelling into beginning reading instruction. In J. L. Metsala & L. C. Ehri (Eds.), *Word recognition in literacy* (pp. 289–313). Mahwah, NJ: Erlbaum.

Treiman, R., & Bourassa, D. C. (2000). The development of spelling skills. *Topics in Language Disorders, 20*(3), 1–18.

Tunley, R. (1957). Johnny can read in Joplin. *Saturday Evening Post, 230*(17), 23, 108–110.

Tyler, R. (1949). *Basic principles of curriculum and instruction.* Chicago: University of Chicago Press.

Urban School Improvement Network. (2010). *Learning walks.* Accessed at http://usinetworkschools.org/our-work/learning-walks on June 1, 2010.

Vaughn, S., Hughes, M. T., Moody, S. W., Elbaum, B. (2001). Instructional grouping for reading for students with LD: Implications for practice. *Intervention in School and Clinic, 36*(3), 131–137.

Vellutino, F., & Scanlon, P. (1987). Phonological coding, phonological awareness, and reading ability: Evidence from a longitudinal and experimental study. *Merrill-Palmer Quarterly, 33,* 321–363.

Vescio, V., Ross, D., & Adams, A. (2008). A review of research on the impact of professional learning communities on teaching practice and student learning. *Teaching and Teacher Education, 24,* 80–91.

Vygotsky, L. S. (1978). *Mind in society: The development of higher psychological processes.* Cambridge, MA: Harvard University Press.

Wade, S. E. (1990). Using think-alouds to assess comprehension. *Reading Teacher, 43*(3), 442–451.

Wagner, R. K., Torgesen, J. K., & Rashotte, C. A. (1994). The development of reading-related phonological processing abilities: New evidence of bi-directional causality from a latent variable longitudinal study. *Developmental Psychology, 30,* 73–87.

Wagner, R. K., Torgesen, J. K., Rashotte, C. A., Hecht, S. A., Barker, T. A., Burgess, S., et al. (1997). Changing causal relations between phonological processing abilities and word-level reading as children develop from beginning to fluent readers: A five-year longitudinal study. *Developmental Psychology, 33,* 468–479.

Walberg, H. J., & Tsai, S. L. (1983). Matthew effects in education. *Educational Research Quarterly, 20,* 359–373.

Walsh, J. A., & Sattes, B. D. (2004). *Quality questioning: Research-based practice to engage every learner.* Thousand Oaks, CA: Corwin Press.

Wang, M. C., Haertel, G. D., & Walberg, H. J. (1993). Toward a knowledge base for school learning. *Review of Educational Research, 63*(3), 249–294.

Wasowicz, J., Apel, K., Masterson, J. & Whitney, A. (2004). *SPELL-Links to reading & writing: A word-study curriculum.* Evanston, IL: Learning By Design.

Weiner, B. (1972). Attribution theory, achievement motivation, and the educational process. *Review of Educational Research, 42*(2), 203–215.

Wharton-McDonald, R., Pressley, M., & Hampston, J. M. (1998). Literacy instruction in nine first-grade classrooms: Teacher characteristics and student achievement. *Elementary School Journal, 99,* 101–128.

Wiggins, G. (1991). Standards, not standardization: Evoking quality student work. *Educational Leadership, 48*(4), 18–25.

Wilhelm, J. D., Baker, T. N., & Dube, J. (2001). *Strategic reading: Guiding students to life-long literacy, 6–12.* Portsmouth, NH: Heinemann.

Willingham, D. (2004). Practice makes perfect: But only if you practice beyond the point of perfection. *American Educator, 28*(1). Accessed at www.aft.org/pubs-reports /american_educator/spring2004/cogsci.html on February 3, 2009.

Willingham, D. (2005). Do visual, auditory, and kinesthetic learners need visual, auditory, and kinesthetic instruction? *American Educator, 29*(2). Accessed at www .aft.org/newspubs/periodicals/ae/summer2005/willingham.cfm on March 8, 2011.

Wong, R. Y. L., Wong, W., Perry, N., & Sawatsky, D. (1986). The efficacy of a self-questioning summarization strategy for use by underachievers and learning disabled adolescents. *Learning Disability Focus, 2,* 20–35.

Wood, D. J., Bruner, J. S., & Ross, G. (1976). The role of tutoring in problem solving. *Journal of Child Psychology and Psychiatry, 17*, 89–100.

Wood, D. J., & Middleton, D. (1975). A study of assisted problem solving. *British Journal of Psychology, 66*, 181–191.

Wood, E. G., Winne, P., & Pressley, M. (1989, April). *Elaborative interrogation, imagery, and provided elaborations as facilitators of children's learning of arbitrary prose.* Paper presented at the American Educational Research Association, New Orleans, LA.

Wood, E., Woloshyn, V. E., & Willoughby, T. (Eds.). (1995). *Cognitive strategy instruction for middle and high schools.* Cambridge, MA: Brookline Books.

Wooden, J. (1997). *Wooden: A lifetime of observations and reflections on and off the court.* Chicago: Contemporary Books.

Yoshida, M. (1999). *Lesson study: An ethnographic investigation of school-based teacher development in Japan.* Unpublished doctoral dissertation, University of Chicago.

Zimmerman, B. J. (1990). Self-regulating academic learning and achievement: The emergence of a social cognitive perspective *Educational Psychology Review, 2*, 173–201.

Zimmerman, B. J. (1998). Developing self-fulfilling cycles of academic regulation: An analysis of exemplary instructional models. In D. Schunk & B. J. Zimmerman (Eds.), *Self-regulated learning: From teaching to self-reflective practice* (pp. 1–19). New York: Guilford Press.

Zimmerman, B. J. (2001). Theories of self-regulated learning and academic achievement: An overview and analysis. In B. J. Zimmerman & D. H. Schunk (Eds.), *Self-regulated learning and academic achievement: Theoretical perspectives* (2nd ed., pp. 1–37). Mahwah, NJ: Erlbaum.

Zimmerman, B. J., & Campillo, M. (2003). Motivating self-regulated problem solvers. In J. E. Davidson & R. J. Sternberg (Eds.), *The psychology of problem solving.* is26_2p. 233–262). Cambridge, England: Cambridge University Press.

Zimmerman, B. J., & Schunk, D. H. (2001). Reflections on theories of self-regulated learning and academic achievement. In D. Schunk & B. J. Zimmerman (Eds.), *Self-regulated learning: From teaching to self-reflective practice* (pp. 289–307). New York: Guilford Press.

Index

communicating vision and mission, 65

creating climate and culture conducive to learning, 64

developing teacher leaders, 66

establishing, implementing, and achieving academic standards, 63–64

establishing and maintaining positive relationships, 66–67

setting high expectations, 65–66

Bloom (1980), 90

Bossidy and Charan (2002), 59

brainstorming

teacher team goal-setting worksheet, 119

brisk instructional pace example, 116

Bryk and Schneider (2002), 70–71, 77

Burns (1978), 77

buy-in

faculty orientations, 76

instructional leadership capacity, 71

C

calculating time needs for walkthroughs, 52–53

categories of look-fors. See understanding look-fors

Center for Comprehensive School Reform and Improvement (2010), 48

Central Union School District, 48

challenges of grade-level walkthroughs, 123–124

challenging teachers, dealing with, 62–63, 70, 89

charts. See posters and charts

checksheet, definition of, 4

City, Elmore, Fiarman, and Teitel (2009), 62, 73

classroom artifacts category

Affinity Process, 84

artifacts definition, 41–42

big idea of, 43

data collection and analysis, 98, 102

description of, 14

exemplars and nonexemplars for, 44–45

introduction, 41–42

look-fors observation protocol, 42

research citations for, 43–44

classroom libraries

classroom artifacts category, 42, 43, 44

climate and culture of school

creating, 64

faculty orientations, 86, 88

trust as factor, 71

climate management

teacher with-it-ness category, 32, 33, 35

coaching during walkthroughs, 56

coaching-facilitating

data collection and analysis, 101, 103

instructional moves category, 16, 18, 21

cognitive aspects of unpacking, 113

cognitive strategies

definition of, 5

lesson template for, 115, 117–118

collaborative planning time, definition of, 5

collaborative teacher teams. See also embedded professional development

action log, 120

definition of, 4

goal-setting worksheet, 119

instructional leadership capacity, 60, 69–70

lack of meeting time, 75

principal visits to meetings, 106

professional standards and, 87

paradigms impacting achievement,
60–62

personal attack, fear of, 62

personal instructional leadership capacity. *See* instructional leadership capacity,
assessing

personnel files, 75, 77

Pfeffer and Sutton (2000), 121, 122

phonemic awareness instruction
student-managed learning activities,
38
teacher-managed instructional activities, 25, 27, 28–29

Pitler and Goodwin (2008), 93

posters and charts
classroom artifacts category, 42, 44,
45
data collection and analysis, 102

Pressley (1998), 1

Primary Commencement ceremony, 129

principal classroom walkthroughs
definition of, 4
understanding classroom walkthroughs, 47–58

principal leadership capacity. *See* instructional leadership capacity, assessing

principal preparation, lack of, 74–75

privacy norms, 124, 125–126

private school data example, 94–99

problem-solving
data analysis and, 94
Force Field Analysis and, 89–90

professional growth. *See also* embedded
professional development
building capacity with walkthroughs,
122–123
faculty orientations, 75, 76, 87
understanding walkthroughs, 48

professional growth unit, definition of, 5

professionalism of teachers

instructional leadership capacity,
62–63
Professional Standards Code process,
86–88

professional learning communities. *See*
collaborative teacher teams

Professional Standards Code process,
86–88, 89

protocol, definition of, 4

purpose-driven instructional moves,
17–18

pushback from teachers
instructional leadership capacity and,
60, 62–63

Q

quality control, checksheets and, 94

quasi-experimental research, definition
of, 5

questioning
instructional moves category, 16, 19,
23

R

reading a lot instruction
student-managed learning activities,
38, 39, 41
teacher-managed instructional activities, 25, 30

reading comprehension instruction. *See*
comprehension instruction

reading log
classroom artifacts category, 42, 44,
45

reading styles, frequently asked questions,
54

recapping
data collection and analysis, 102
instructional moves category, 16, 19,
23

record keeping

40 Reading Intervention Strategies for K–6 Students
Research-Based Support for RTI
Elaine K. McEwan-Adkins
This well-rounded collection of reading intervention strategies, teacher-friendly lesson plans, and adaptable miniroutines will support and inform your RTI efforts. Many of the strategies motivate all students as well as scaffold struggling readers. Increase effectiveness by using the interventions across grade-level teams or schoolwide.
BKF270

Teaching Reading & Comprehension to English Learners, K–5
Margarita Calderón
Raise achievement for English learners through new instructional strategies and assessment processes. This book addresses the language, literacy, and content instructional needs of ELs and frames quality instruction within effective schooling structures and the implementation of RTI.
BKF402

Literacy 2.0
Reading and Writing in 21st Century Classrooms
Nancy Frey, Douglas Fisher, and Alex Gonzalez
Students in the 21st century must incorporate traditional literacy skills into a mastery of technology for communicating and collaborating in new ways. This book offers specific teaching strategies for developing students' skills related to acquiring, producing, and sharing information.
BKF373

Power Tools for Adolescent Literacy
Strategies for Learning
Jan Rozzelle and Carol Scearce
This comprehensive collection of powerful literacy tools and strategies for middle school teachers is based on research from top literacy experts.
BKF261

a division of

Solution Tree | Press
Solution Tree

Visit solution-tree.com or call 800.733.6786 to order.